Series / Number 07-066

Q METHODOLOGY

BRUCE McKEOWN
Seattle Pacific University

DAN THOMAS
Wartburg College

SAGE PUBLICATIONS
The International Professional Publishers
Newbury Park   London   New Delhi

For information address:

SAGE Publications, Inc.
2455 Teller Road
Newbury Park, California 91320

SAGE Publications Ltd.
6 Bonhill Street
London EC2A 4PU
United Kingdom

SAGE Publications India Pvt. Ltd.
M-32 Market
Greater Kailash I
New Delhi 110 048 India

International Standard Book Number 0-8039-2753-3

Library of Congress Catalog Card No. 87-042926

93 94 15 14 13 12 11 10 9 8 7 6 5 4

When citing a university paper, please use the proper form. Remember to cite the correct
Sage University Paper series title and include the paper number. One of the following
formats can be adapted (depending on the style manual used):

(1) IVERSEN, GUDMUND R. and NORPOTH, HELMUT (1976) "Analysis of
Variance." Sage University Paper series on Quantitative Applications in the Social
Sciences, 07-001. Beverly Hills: Sage Pubns.

OR

(2) Iversen, Gudmund R. and Norpoth, Helmut. 1976. *Analysis of Variance.* Sage
University Paper series on Quantitative Applications in the Social Sciences, series no.
07-001. Beverly Hills: Sage Pubns.

CONTENTS

SERIES EDITOR'S INTRODUCTION

Subjectivity—an individual's personal point of view—is sometimes thought to be impossible to study systematically or with any degree of precision. Not so, Q methodology—commonly and incompletely known as the Q-sorting technique—encompasses a distinctive set of psychometric and operational principles that, when combined with specialized statistical applications of correlational and factor-analytical techniques, provide researchers with a systematic and rigorously quantitative means for examining human subjectivity. Q methodology is based on the twofold premise that subjective points-of-view are communicable and always advanced from a position of self-reference. As such, subjective communication is amenable to objective analysis and understanding provided that the analytical means for studying such communications do not in the process destroy or alter their self-referent properties. Thus, central to Q methodology is a concern with ensuring that self-reference is preserved rather than compromised by or confused with an external frame of reference brought by an investigator.

Q Methodology, by Bruce McKeown and Dan Thomas, outlines the various principles, techniques, and procedures through which these premises are advanced. Their coverage includes discussions of data-gathering procedures (e.g., Q-samples and Q-sorting) and statistical techniques (e.g., factor analysis), as well as strategies for conducting small-sample behavioral research along Q-methodological lines. In doing so, they strive for balanced coverage of technical procedures along with the methodological and philosophical perspectives that make this method distinctive.

As an introductory primer, *Q Methodology* also provides ample points of departure for entry into the detailed technical and substantive literature on Q-method. Given the ubiquity of and yet elusive nature of subjectivity in the subject matter of the social sciences, the authors emphasize issues of practical applicability to illustrate the promise and relevance of Q methodology to disciplines as diverse as psychology, sociology and political science.

—*Richard G. Niemi*
Series Co-Editor

SYNOPSIS

Commonly (and incompletely) known as the "Q-sorting technique," Q methodology encompasses a distinctive set of psychometric and operational principles that, when conjoined with specialized statistical applications of correlational and factor-analytical techniques, provides researchers a systematic and rigorously quantitative means for examining human subjectivity. From the standpoint of Q methodology, subjectivity is regarded simply as a person's point of view on any matter of personal and/or social importance. Corollary to this conception is the twofold premise that subjective points of view are "communicable" and always advanced from a position of "self reference." Thus construed, subjective communication is amenable to "objective analysis" and understanding *provided that* the analytical means for rendering such communications objective do not in the process destroy or alter the self-referent properties of such communications. Central to Q methodology is a concern—fortified by operational and statistical specificities—to ensure that self-reference is preserved rather than compromised by, or confused with, an external frame of reference brought by an investigator in seeking to measure subjective phenomena. This monograph outlines the various principles, techniques, and procedures through which this methodological ambition is advanced. Included herein are discussions of data-gathering instrumentation (e.g., Q-samples and Q-sorting), statistical techniques of analysis (e.g., Q-factor analysis), and strategies for conducting small sample behavioral research along Q-methodological lines. As an introductory primer, the monograph provides ample points of departure for entry into the larger, more detailed technical, as well as substantive, literature on Q-method. Given the ubiquity yet elusiveness of subjectivity in the subject matter of the social sciences, issues of practical applicability are emphasized to illustrate the promise and relevance of Q methodology to disciplines as diverse as psychology, social psychology, sociology, and political science.

PREFACE

The word *methodology* in the title underscores a premise and a purpose of this monograph. The premise is that "Q" is a methodology, and it is within this larger methodological framework that the significance of Q-sorting—the key technical component of an inclusive logic of inquiry—is best understood. The purpose, signaled also by the word "introduction," is thus methodological and not only procedural in nature. This does not mean that the kinds of practical "how to do it" treatments that characterize other QASS volumes are missing or given short shrift. On the contrary, we have attempted to introduce the methodology in such a way that it will be intelligible to the uninitiated "novice." And toward this end we demonstrate, to the extent that space limitations allow, important methodological principles and complex procedures with examples from actual research. Nevertheless, we believe that no matter how "introductory," a primer on Q methodology should be nothing less than that—a reasonably complete treatment of the method *as a method*.

Our aim in making this clear at the outset stems from our concern that a good deal of confusion over the nature and value of the approach to subjectivity that we describe has arisen over the mistaken notion that Q methodology involves little more than the application of the Q-sorting technique in addressing a research problem. There are noteworthy exceptions, to be sure, but in the vast majority of the more than 1,500 entries that make up the literature in which applications and discussions of Q appear, precious little attention is given to broader methodological foundations and principles. In part this may be due to the view that such issues frequently are regarded as controversial. With this we do not disagree. As a methodology, Q embraces a distinctive orientation toward the systematic study of human subjectivity. Defined as much by a particular logic of inquiry as by technical specificities, this orientation is frequently and undeniably at odds with conventional "R-methodological" approaches to the measurement and study of subjective phenomena such as opinions, attitudes, and values.

9

To the extent possible, we seek in this volume to steer a middle course between two extreme, counterproductive courses of direction that seem to follow from this (alleged) distinctiveness. On the one hand, we must guard against overzealousness: Distinctiveness is often taken to imply superiority and, whether the latter is intended or not, researchers convinced of Q's virtuosity, ourselves included, are certainly not immune to the temptations of *hubris*. While important differences between Q and R do exist, and while these differences almost inevitably give rise to contention over "which is right and which cause is therefore just," we know from personal experience that vigorous efforts toward methodological elucidation share a very thin border with self-righteous and pretentious forms of methodological evangelism. On the other hand, there is little to be gained from soft-pedaling or neglecting entirely methodological distinctiveness in the interest of avoiding charges of undue contentiousness in the service of advocacy.

How well we are able to find, let alone steer, such a middle course is left for our readers to decide. In so doing, we believe that they will be best served if they are enabled to assess the character, contribution, and merits of Q methodology. And in this regard, the true test of any methodology is to be found, pragmatically, in the veritable pudding of what it produces: what it brings to light and the intensity of the illumination it affords.

Topically, the monograph is organized into five sections or chapters. The first provides an initial overview, introducing concepts and principles with illustrations drawn from research on an issue of public opinion. Basic principles and techniques of Q-sample construction, Q-sorting mechanics, and the role of conditions of instruction (matters pertinent to data collection) are discussed in Chapter 2. The third chapter addresses the issue of respondent selection and the specific manner in which single case analyses are given theoretical fortification within the Q-method framework. The statistical procedures by which Q-sort data are analyzed are treated in Chapter 4. Finally, we conclude with two rather extended examples, illustrating the utility of Q-method in research applications of diverse substantive and theoretical interest.

Q METHODOLOGY

BRUCE McKEOWN
Seattle Pacific University

DAN THOMAS
Wartburg College

1. INTRODUCTORY OVERVIEW

Introduction and Purpose

Now more than a half century old (Stephenson, 1935), Q methodology can hardly lay claim to the status of a "new" or "innovative" strategy for conducting behavioral research. Indeed, the literature on Q methodology now contains more than 1,500 bibliographic entries (Brown, 1986), and journals reporting research from Q-studies can be found across the social sciences spectrum, both inside and out of the English-speaking world. Be that as it may, Q retains a somewhat fugitive status within the larger social scientific community. Our purpose in this primer is not to belabor this characteristic, but simply to describe the method and its techniques, which, taken in their entirety, set Q apart as a complete and distinctive approach with its own principles for analyzing human behavior. Our aim, in short, is to introduce the philosophy and illustrate the procedural steps by which Q-technique and its methodology can be employed in behavioral research.

In addition to theoretical and task-related purposes for considering Q, the method can be recommended for several reasons. Q-method typically employs small numbers of respondents and the in-depth study of single cases is not uncommon. The reasons for this, as we shall see, are broadly philosophical rather than narrowly pragmatic. Yet, as a practical matter, Q-technique makes rigorous methods available to those lacking hefty

11

research budgets and the computer facilities necessary for the analysis of large data sets. Given the ubiquitous presence of personal computers and relatively low-cost "main frame" statistics programs to accompany them (e.g., SPSS/PC and SYSTAT), Q-studies can be readily conducted by anyone with a basic knowledge of research statistics.

Subjectivity and Self-Reference

Fundamentally, Q entails a method for the scientific study of human subjectivity.[1] Subjectivity, in the lexicon of Q methodology, means nothing more than a *person's communication of his or her point of view*. As such, subjectivity is always anchored in *self-reference,* that is, the person's "internal" frame of reference, but this does not render it inaccessible to rigorous examination. Nor does it serve to reify the self in any metaphysical or phenomenological sense. Self-referent subjectivity of this sort, on the contrary, is "pure behavior" (Brown, 1980: 46), and it is at issue anytime an individual remarks, "It seems to me . . . " or "In my opinion . . . ." In speaking thus, an individual is saying something meaningful about personal experience, and what Q methodology provides is a systematic means to examine and reach understandings about such experience. Toward this end, the respondent's frame of reference is preserved. Q-studies, from conception to completion, adhere to the methodological axiom that *subjectivity is always self-referent.* As Brown (1986: 58) has said: "Only subjective opinions are at issue in Q, and although they are typically unprovable, they can nevertheless be shown to have structure and form, and it is the task of Q-technique to make this form manifest for purposes of observation and study."

As a matter of principle, then, Q methodology would seem to hold special promise for those seeking to make more intelligible and rigorous the study of human subjectivity. In the Q-methodological pursuit of this end, the researcher seeks to model—or, more accurately, enables the respondent to model his or her—viewpoints on a matter of subjective importance through the operational medium of a Q-sort. This "modeling" is accomplished by a respondent systematically rank-ordering a purposively sampled set of stimuli, namely, a Q-sample, according to a specific condition of instruction (e.g., from those that are "most characteristic of my viewpoint" to those that are "most uncharacteristic of my viewpoint"). The nature of the stimuli making up the Q-sample is constrained only by the domain of subjectivity in which the researcher is interested (a domain that Stephenson [1978b] has termed a "communication concourse").

Once viewpoints are modeled in Q-sorts, data analysis occurs with the intercorrelations of the N Q-sorts as variables (hence persons, not traits or Q-sample items, are correlated) and *factor analysis* of the $N \times N$ correlation matrix. Resulting factors represent points of view, and the association of each respondent with each point of view is indicated by the magnitude of his or her *loading* on that factor. The final step in data analysis involves the calculation of factor scores, whereby each statement (or stimulus element) in the Q-sample is "scored" for each factor. Factor scoring aids the task of understanding and interpreting the meanings of the factors in two ways: first, through the construction of a *factor array* (a composite Q-sort, one for each factor), and second, through the determination of statements whose ranks in the arrays are statistically different for any pair of given factors. Finally, interpretation of the factors is advanced in terms of consensual and divergent subjectivity, with attention given to the relevance of such patterns to existing or emerging theories, propositions, and the like.

An Illustration: Perspectives on Gay Rights

To illustrate, we consider the controversy regarding homosexuality in American society. A citywide initiative campaign in Seattle, Washington, was recently mounted to repeal the inclusion of "sexual orientation" protection in open housing and fair employment policies. The initiative drive generated an intense public debate from which many different opinions were sampled.

To examine the conflict, a sample of opinions was drawn from over 200 statements collected from diverse sources, including letters to the editor, newspaper and magazine reports, "person in the street" interviews, editorial positions, and television talk shows. Although some issue dimensions were readily apparent, such as direction (pro and con), others became clear only after the statement population was studied in detail. Concerns were expressed about moral and social issues, the consequences of homosexual lifestyles, the impact of homosexuality upon traditional institutions and values, the value of social pluralism, and so on.

To reduce the opinion items to a manageable number yet ensure that those selected were representative (Brunswick, 1956) of the content of the debate, statements were chosen according to the design presented in Figure 1.1. (This and other procedures are discussed at length in subsequent sections.) The dimensions or criteria built into the design reflected issues occurring in the public debate. Therefore, the final sample of stimulus

Main Effects	Components		N
A. Direction	(a) Pro-Gay Rights	(b) Anti-Gay Rights	2
B. Dimensions	(c) Moral	(d) Civil	2
C. Issues	(e) Consequences	(f) Institutional Values	
	(g) Behavior	(h) Social Pluralism	
	(i) Minority Status		5

Q Sample = (Main Effects)(Replications) = ([A][B][C])(m)

(A)(B)(C) = (2)(2)(5) = 20 combinations:

$$
\begin{array}{ll}
ace & bce \\
acf & bcf \\
acg & bcg \\
ach & bch \\
aci & bci \\
ade & bde \\
adf & bdf \\
adg & bdg \\
adh & bdh \\
adi & bdi \\
\end{array}
$$

Replications (m) = 3

$\underline{N}$ = (2)(2)(5)(3) = 60 Q-sample statements

Figure 1.1: Q-Sample Design for a Homosexual Rights Q-Study

statements, or *Q-sample,* was composed of opinions matching the design combinations. In order to expand the coverage of expressions, each of the 20 combinations was replicated three times for a final Q-sample of 60 items.

It was decided, for example, that the following was a comment representative of a Pro-Gay Rights-Moral-Consequences position (combination *ace* in Figure 1.1):

The Biblical and moral questions raised by the issue of homosexuality are sufficiently vague to cloud the issue. Therefore, to predict dire moral consequences following from gay rights is unfair since we are not sure what is involved in the first place.

An Anti-Civil-Minority Status (*bdi*) view was reflected in the following:

Gays, like felons or drug pushers, do not deserve minority status protection since they are not a true minority based on color of skin or nationality.

An Anti-Moral-Behavior (*bcg*) position is expressed in the following opinion:

Just the thought of somebody participating in a homosexual act is disgusting and morally offensive.

Whereas, from the other point of view (*ach*), the opinion was given as follows:

The danger posed by anti-gay rights movements is that they are just recent attempts to legislate and regulate morality and shove private convictions down everybody's throats.

Some 53 persons rank-ordered the 60 statement items by sorting them from +5 to –5 according to the distribution presented in Figure 2.2. These rankings (i.e., Q-sorts) were correlated and then factor analyzed to discover the groupings of opinions as expressed among the respondents. Three factors, that is, three distinct clusters of opinions, emerged with all 53 respondents identified with one or more of the three perspectives. A portion of the factor matrix is shown in Table 1.1. Contained therein are factor coefficients (factor loadings) across the three factors for half of the respondents. Subjects 1 through 5 "define" Factor A, that is, each has a statistically significant loading, ranging from +.75 to +.80, on Factor A and insignificant loadings (lower than +/−.33) on the other two (criteria for determining significant loadings and other technical matters are discussed in Section 4). Subject 5 is a slight exception: He apparently shares the Factor C attitude but not in a significant way (+.24). Otherwise, subjects 6 through 14 are clearly associated with Factor B and subjects 15, 16, and 17 are found on Factor C. The remaining respondents are scattered across the factors or, as in the case of subjects 18 through 21, are positively associated with Factor A but bipolar (negatively loaded) on Factor B.

TABLE 1.1
Factor Matrix for Selected Subjects from Gay Rights Q-Study

S	FACTOR* A	B	C	SEX	AGE	OCCUPATION	PARTY	RELIGION	VOTE?+
1	80	08	02	M	20	student	---	Baptist	N
2	79	05	-07	F	23	sect'y	---	Evangelical	N
3	77	-07	-13	F	52	nurse-ed	Rep	Free Meth	N
4	76	-06	16	M	17	student	Ind	Presbty'an	N
5	75	14	24	M	26	professor	---	---	N
6	02	86	04	M	18	student	Rep	Protestant	Y
7	06	84	03	F	43	writer	Rep	Christian	Y
8	-09	84	02	M	25	student	Ind	Protestant	?
9	-13	83	02	M	18	student	Rep	Protestant	Y
10	-19	82	21	M	18	student	Cons	Protestant	Y
11	-20	81	04	M	18	student	Rep	Protestant	Y
12	-02	78	04	M	18	student	Rep	Protestant	Y
13	-07	70	18	F	59	professor	Rep	Presbty'an	Y
14	-02	67	-08	M	19	student	Rep	Assmb.God	N
15	22	-28	61	M	19	student	Rep	Lutheran	?
16	26	01	61	F	20	student	---	Protestant	Y
17	13	23	35	M	18	student	Ind	Jewish	Y
18	73	-34	23	F	45	professor	---	Christian	N
19	68	-54	02	M	23	staff	Dem	Non-denom	N
20	63	-59	22	F	57	professor	Dem	Methodist	N
21	62	-52	19	F	39	professor	Dem	Presbty'an	N

(continued)

TABLE 1.1 (continued)

22	-33	65	42	F	18	student	Cons	---	Y
23	-26	47	41	M	21	student.	---	Christian	N
24	-31	46	60	M	58	administ	Dem	Free Meth	Y
25	45	18	56	F	21	student	Dem	---	-
26	56	-50	40	M	46	professor	---	Lutheran	N
27	42	-06	44	F	20	student	---	Rmn Cath	?

```
*Decimals to two places have been omitted. Factor loadings
 +/-.33 are significant p<.01.
⁺The following question was included on the Q sort score sheet:
 If you had the opportunity to vote on repealing "gay-rights"
 protection laws, would you vote to repeal or not?
```

In Q-method, variables are the people performing the Q-sorts, not Q-sample statements. Persons significantly associated with a given factor, therefore, are assumed to share a common perspective. Hence, from among the many thousands of possible combinations, the 60 Q-sample items were sorted by the five people defining Factor A essentially in the same way. In the original matrix of Pearson product-moment correlations, the inter-correlations of their Q-sorts were sufficiently high that they were grouped separately, in the factor analysis, from the other respondents. Therefore, each respondent's factor "loading" indicates the degree of association between that person's individual Q-sort and the underlying composite attitude or perspective of the factor. *In Q methodology the presence of several orthogonal (independent) factors is evidence of different points of view in the person-sample. An individual's positive loading on a factor indicates his or her shared subjectivity with others on that factor; negative loadings, on the other hand, are signs of rejection of the factor's perspective.*

We can now briefly consider the meanings of the factors. (A more detailed presentation of Q-study results and technical procedures is found in Section 5.) Factors can be interpreted by referring to demographic correlates of the respondents (Table 1.1) and, more importantly, to the *factor scores* for each factor. Factor scores are essentially weighted z-scores for each statement in the Q-sample; these can be reconverted into an array of scores (factor array) corresponding to the +5 to –5 values used in the original Q-sort continuum (computational equations for factor weights, factor scores, and factor arrays are presented and discussed in Section 4). Space limitations preclude reproduction of the entire Q-sample, but by examining the factor scores for selected items we can discern the basic themes distinguishing the three perspectives (Table 1.2).

Statement scores for the factors show that Factors A and C are alike in the importance attached to the principle of social tolerance in the context of competing lifestyles and conflicting values. In this respect, they share a traditional "liberal" orientation, as reflected in statements 8 and 23 (scores in parentheses for Factors A, B, and C, respectively).

> 8. The issue is not whether or not ours is going to be a free society. If it is we will have to allow people to make choices that we may feel are wrong or immoral or sinful. (+5 –2 +1)

> 23. There is nothing wrong with trying to understand and/or tolerate others people's homosexuality. Even if it violates the Bible and gives you the "willies," there is nothing wrong with trying to understand the people who live that way. (+3 –1 +1)

When such consensual items are viewed contextually, however, it becomes clear that the liberalism linking Factors A and C and distinguishing them from Factor B is not altogether of one piece. While both affirm, as a general principle, that toleration for minority viewpoints and lifestyles is essential, Factor A extends this principle to include members of the gay community, whereas Factor C does not.

> 18. The majority of the people in the United States should not have to be subjected to, or cater to, the rantings of the minority groups when they reflect badly on the beliefs of Christians. (–2 0 +2)

> 25. Gays do not deserve minority status protection—they are not members of a true minority based on color of skin or nationality. They don't qualify for minority status just like prostitutes or pimps or felons or drug pushers don't qualify as minorities. (–2 +3 +3)

Although in agreement with A on other issues, Factor C overtly rejects the homosexuals' claim as a minority group. In this respect, Factor C and

Factor B are alike: *On this issue,* they oppose Factor A's assertion that the central question raised by the gay rights controversy is civil libertarian and, to be consistent, that gays are entitled to the same civil rights safeguards as other minority groups:

16. On this issue of "gay rights" it seems to me the question of civil rights has wrongly been brought into what is a moral issue. (−3 +1 +1)

Factors B and C are at odds, however, when the theological-moral dimension is raised. The distinguishing characteristic of Factor B is opposition to homosexuality because of its sinful nature. The inherent immorality (no. 3) and its social consequences (no. 14) override any consideration of civil rights (no. 34) or toleration (nos. 23 and 53). On these points, Factor B takes issue with the other two.

14. Homosexuality is a sin and homosexual teachers will destroy the American family. The American way of life will disappear if they continue to teach our young. (−4 +1 −5)

34. Sometimes too much talk just clouds the issue. The simple matter is homosexuality is not a civil rights issue but a moral one where the law of the Bible and tradition is clear: it is wrong! (0 +5 +1)

53. It's time we faced up to the fact that sin is sin, that homosexuality is sin and God does not tolerate it. Neither should we. (0 +4 −4)

Thus, in contradistinction to the social liberalism of Factors A and C, Factor B is centered within a theologically conservative framework. The "conservative" perspective is indicated, too, by the subjects' party identification (mainly Republican) and their desire to repeal gay rights protection ordinances (see Table 1.1). Factor A and C respondents tend to identify themselves either as Democrats or as independents and they have been previously supportive of legal protection.

One other dimension deserves comment. The homosexual issue seems to create several cross-pressures so that all three viewpoints are qualified by a degree of ambivalence. All of the respondents are active members of an evangelical Christian community and identify with a religious tradition affirming certain moral proscriptions but also a history of charitable social involvement. Sensitive to the cross-pressures produced by this tradition, the conservative Factor B, while resolute on the "sin" issue, hesitates to deny all human rights. This is indicated by uncertainty in some statement scores (e.g., by the 0 rank for item 18, noted above) and by the mild disagreement with others, including statement 28:

TABLE 1.2
Factor Scores for Selected Statements from Gay Rights Q-Sample

	FACTOR		
	A	B	C
3. God created male and female in His image. What an abomination homosexuality is to God's plan.	0	+5	-1
8. The issue is not whether or not homosexuality is a sin. The issue is whether or not ours is going to be a free society. If it is we will have to allow people to make choices that we may feel are wrong or immoral or sinful.	+5	-2	+1
14. Homosexuality is a sin and homosexual teachers will destroy the American family. The American way of life will disappear if they continue to teach our young.	-4	1	-5
16. On this issue of "gay rights" it seems to me the question of civil rights has been wrongly brought into what is a moral issue.	-3	+1	+1
18. The majority of the people in the United States should not have to be subjected to, or cater to, the rantings of the minority groups when they reflect badly on the beliefs of Christians.	-2	0	+2
23. There is nothing wrong with trying to understand and/or tolerate other people's homosexuality. Even if it violates the Bible and gives you the "willies" there is nothing wrong with trying to understand the people who live that way.	+3	-1	+1

(continued)

TABLE 1.2 (continued)

25. Gays do not deserve minority status protection—— they are not members of a true minority based on color of skin or nationality. They don't qualify for minority status just like prostitutes or pimps or felons or drug pushers don't qualify as minorities.	-2	+3	+3
28. City ordinances preventing discrimination against homosexuals do not grant special rights but ensure that the right to a job and place to live are maintained for all citizens. Even if one considers homosexuality unChristian one should be in favor of these rights.	+5	-1	-2
34. Sometimes too much talk just clouds the issue. The simple matter is homosexuality is not a civil rights issue but a moral one where the law of the Bible and tradition is clear: it is wrong!	0	+5	+1
43. Christians should encourage homosexuals to enter into permanent loving relationships rather than fail at heterosexual marriages or impersonal sexual encounters.	-5	-5	-2
53. It's time we faced up to the fact that sin is sin, that homosexuality is sin and God does not tolerate it. Neither should we.	0	+5	-4

City ordinances preventing discrimination against homosexuals do not grant special rights but ensure that the right to a job and place to live are maintained for all citizens. Even if one considers homosexuality unChristian, one should be in favor of these rights. (+5 – 1 – 2)

Likewise, Factor A is unclear about some of the theological-moral issues (no. 3: God created male and female in His image. What an abomination homosexuality is to God's plan. [0 +5 –1]).

All three factors agree that there are limits to toleration. They deny, for example, the wisdom of encouraging homosexual relationships as an alternative to other possibilities:

> 43. Christians should encourage homosexuals to enter into permanent loving relationships rather than fail at heterosexual marriages or impersonal sexual encounters. (−5 −5 −2)

Whereas one would expect this of Factor B, it also suggests that Factor A respondents, given their uncertainties, feel less discomfort, perhaps, in tolerating and distinguishing between competing values. In this respect, Factor A "makes sense" as a naturally occurring (or, "operant") facsimile of the neoorthodox Christian perspective, exemplified by Reinhold Niebuhr in *The Children of Light and the Children of Darkness* (1944: viii):

> Man's capacity for justice makes democracy possible; but man's inclination to injustice makes democracy necessary.

Methodological Issues

The "gay rights" study illustrates the meaning of *operant subjectivity*. A key finding, as noted, is that tolerance assumes importance, albeit in different ways, for two of the three positions. For Factor B, in contrast, other matters are more crucial (e.g., the nature of sin) and eclipse civil libertarian or social pluralist considerations so important to Factors A and C. Tolerance therefore emerges as a thematic interpretation in consequence of the respondents' Q-sorting operations: *No definition is assumed beforehand but is inferred from the location of statements provided by the respondent as he or she distributes them along the Q-sort continuum*. To be sure, subjectivity is implicated whenever an attempt is made to interpret and so attribute meaning to a respondent's behavior. What distinguishes Q methodology from conventional measurement strategies in this regard are the temporal locus of and inferential bases for this attribution.

First, in contradistinction to conventional R-methodological practice, a concept such as tolerance is not assumed to have a priori meaning apart from and independently of the respondent's self-reference. If it did, a scale could be employed so as to align respondents on a single continuum of social tolerance. Assuming adequate reliability and validity, and depending on whether the scale's specific items included reference to homosexuals as objects of tolerance or intolerance, one may or may not conclude that Factor A and Factor C types are tolerant whereas Factor B types are not.

The problem with this approach is that it introduces arbitrary subjectivity—in this case, the social scientist's—in an a prior way into the measurement process. Respondents are either tolerant or intolerant in greater or lesser degrees by virtue of the researcher's categorical operational definition. Categorical definitions always carry the risk of missing or misinterpreting meaning from the respondent's own frame of reference. The point is that tolerance, just like the issues and events that elicit concerns about it, is amenable to individually determined definitions drawn from personal experiences. As such, it is subject to a host of meanings, each of which may well be "sensible" from the standpoint of the respondent's own logic.

Second, the gay rights study illustrates the importance of *contextuality,* especially as it relates to factor interpretation. The qualitative differences distinguishing Factor A from Factor C versions of tolerance are revealed contextually, not in terms of the placement of one or two statements read in isolation from the rest. The principle of contextuality is tied to self-reference and also to Q's premises as a *method of impression,* as opposed to expression (Beebe-Center, 1929). This point deserves brief elaboration, since the impression versus expression distinction lies at the heart of the differences between Q- and R-method.

Under methods of *expression,* respondents are measured for traits, attitudes, and the like from an *external* point of view. The respondent's own point of view on the matter is of little theoretical interest and technical significance. For example, from responses to items on the F-scale, a subject receives a score indicating his or her level of authoritarianism. The meanings that the items of the scale may hold for the subject, and the intentions implicit when responding to them, are of no interest to the investigator; these, allegedly, have been predetermined and validated prior to the scale's implementation (see Brunner, 1977). With methods of *impression,* on the other hand, the personal, intraindividual significance of "test stimuli" is of primary importance. When responding to them, the *subject assigns* scores in terms of some relevant conditions that bear, in one way or another, on his or her *internal* frame of reference.

Which set of methods is most appropriate is a matter determined by the research task at hand. Generally speaking, when capabilities or objective behavioral performances are at issue—as in the customary study of intelligence, for example—methods of expression are in order. When the focus is on subjectivity—as in the gay rights study—methods of impression are indicated.

The importance of contextuality in Q methodology stems directly from its status as a method of impression. When speaking of contextuality, we are also addressing a corollary of self-reference: Having no inherent meaning or status as facts, individual items in a Q-sample are assigned meaning and significance, first in Q-sorting by the respondent, and second, in factor interpretation by the researcher. Such assignment is rendered sensible as part of a pattern or configuration of meaning. The ascription of meaning, furthermore, is not supplied from the outside since factors are operant representations of whole perspectives rather than analytically distinct traits synthesized within the researcher's frame of reference (Brown, 1972).

This point can be made with a final illustration. Suppose four stimuli, arrayed below in the left-hand column, form a miniscale of political values, and that subjects A and B complete the scale by responding, *ad seriatim,* in a yes-or-no fashion in the same way as shown.

	Yes	*No*
(1) human rights	A, B	
(2) property rights	A, B	
(3) communism		A, B
(4) fascism		A, B

Their identical responses would seem to indicate a shared "liberal" ideology. However, if we changed the behavioral task and asked them to rank the items vis-à-vis one another, the results could well be the following:

	A	*B*
(Most Agree With)	1	2
	2	1
	3	4
(Least Agree With)	4	3

In terms of political values, individual A is now clearly of the political left, whereas B is closer to the right. Two people passing as ideological twins on the yes-or-no scale, upon closer scrutiny afforded by a slight but significant methodological alteration, are actually political opponents. In this fashion, contextuality clarifies what by definition and design is unclear at the outset of a Q-study: how respondents' themselves, quite apart from the researcher's preconceptions, define the world about them.

2. Q-SAMPLES, Q-SORTING, AND CONDITIONS
OF INSTRUCTION

Q-Samples

A Q-sample is a collection of stimulus items—such as the 60 statements related to the gay rights issue—that is presented to respondents for rank-ordering in a Q-sort. Types of Q-samples can be distinguished in a number of ways. For convenience we employ two distinctions, noting first the differences between "naturalistic" and "ready-made" samples and, second, the contrast between those that are "structured" or "unstructured" by design. Statements taken from respondents' oral or written communications are naturalistic. Those drawn from sources other than their own communications are ready-made. Items from both also can be combined in hybrid samples. Neither is inherently superior to the other; one should select the type best suited to the research at hand.

Naturalistic Q-samples. The advantage of naturalistic Q-samples is twofold: (1) They mirror the opinions of the persons performing the Q-sorts, and (2) they expedite both the Q-sorting process and the attributions of meaning since the items are based upon the respondents' own communications. Given these origins, naturalistic Q-samples greatly reduce the risk of missing the respondents' meanings or confusing them with alternative meanings deriving from an external frame of reference.

Naturalistic Q-samples can be devised in several ways. *Interviewing* is most consistent with the principle of self-reference. It also facilitates single case studies: During the interviews, persons, objects, symbols, and events, in addition to statements, can be identified and incorporated in future conditions of instruction for subsequently administered Q-sorts. The major drawback of interviewing is inconvenience: Interviews require more time and effort than many subjects are willing to invest.

Illustrative of the interview approach to generating Q-samples is a study by Ricks (1972; also see Brown, 1981) of a man who, during life history interviews, identified many people who figured prominently in his life. Instead of sampling opinion statements, Ricks extracted 76 names from the interview protocols and these in turn were placed in a Q-sample that the subject then sorted under 19 different conditions of instruction (e.g., "from those who had the greatest amount of influence upon my life to those who had the least").

When interviews are not feasible, Q-samples can be collected from written narratives. McKeown and Craig (1978) analyzed reactions of

American college students to their educational experiences at a foreign university. In previous years, students wrote extensive evaluations of their educational, social, and cultural encounters and reactions. Statements representative of a variety of reactions were taken from the essays and put into a Q-sample. Students participating in the program at a later date completed the 42-item "Culture Awareness Q-sort" under pretest and post-test conditions.

In another example, Brown (1977) examined responses to political literature by having students read political novels and write reports expressing their personal reactions to the novels' characters and political themes. Statements were sampled from the essays. The final Q-sample consisted of 54 statements and these were returned to the readers, whose task was to model their individual opinions of the novel. Other research based on respondent essays is reported by Martin and Taylor (1978) and by Thomas, Martin, Taylor, and Baas (1984) in connection with the study of political obligation, and by Stephenson (1978a) in an investigation of audience responses to movies.

Another alternative to the interview approach exploits secondary sources such as newspaper editorials, letters to the editor, television and radio talk shows, and the like. The gay rights Q-sample is one example. Such Q-samples are naturalistic since items are taken from real-world communication contexts.

Ready-made Q-samples. As the label implies, item samples of this type derive from sources other than the communications of respondents. Several subtypes are available: quasi-naturalistic Q-samples, Q-samples drawn from conventional rating scales, standardized Q-sorts, and a "hybrid" category.

Quasi-naturalistic Q-samples are similar to those drawn from interviews but are developed from sources external to the study. Brown (1970a), for example, conjoined Q-technique with experimentation to demonstrate ideological persistence on the part of the politically unsophisticated, thereby challenging the conventional portrait of the mass public as incapable of ideological thought (Converse, 1964). In this case, Q-sample statements were taken from Lane's (1962) in-depth interviews with 15 working-class men on issues of enduring political relevance and were supplemented with some of Lane's concluding remarks. In another study, Brown (1974d) sampled 54 statements representative of the three types of "social consciousness" outlined in Charles Reich's (1971) treatise on social character. The three factors that emerged corroborated Reich's ideal typical formulations, although unexpected nuances of meaning qualified his a priori conceptualizations in important ways.

For methodological reasons, *standardized scales* are generally de-emphasized, but they need not be discarded. Items borrowed from attitude and attribute scales can be incorporated into Q-samples to examine whether personal meanings held by respondents comport with the meanings that the items are designed to measure. The use of conventional scale items does not preclude the discovery of meanings different from those "built into" the scale. Conventional scales designed to assess ideological position across the Left-Right spectrum were used by Thomas (1978, 1979) to compose a Political Ideology Q-sample. His findings, however, discussed more fully elsewhere in this work, showed ideological opponents not to be located at opposite ends of the same continuum, but at extreme poles of orthogonal factors.

Also illustrative in this regard are a number of studies employing the "Likability Q-sample" (Baas, 1979; McKeown, 1977; Thomas, 1979; Thomas and Sigelman, 1984; Thomas, Sigelman and Baas, 1984). In these cases, Q-sample items were drawn from Anderson's (1968) compilation of 555 personality-descriptive traits, stratified according to their relative social desirability. In addition, mood adjective checklists (Nowlis, 1965; Lorr, Daston, and Smith, 1967) have been converted into Q-samples to explore the affective dimensions of interpersonal and symbolic objects previously described with the Anderson Q-samples (see, e.g., Brown, 1982, 1983; McKeown, 1978; Baas, 1979).

Other conventional rating scales also have been adopted (e.g., scales of alienation, self-esteem, locus of control, authoritarianism, "Machiavellianism," religiosity, and so on) by treating the items as Q-sample statements. Brown and Rothenberg's (1976) "Interpersonal Perception Method" Q-sort, based on Laing, Phillipson, and Lee (1966), exemplifies this approach as does Thomas's (1976) use of items from the "polarity scale" (Tomkins, 1965) to form an "ideo-affective postures" Q-sample.

Hybrid types. Items from naturalistic and ready-made Q-samples can be combined to form hybrid types. Examples include Brown and Ellithorp's (1970) study of supporters of Eugene McCarthy, Brown's (1974c) analysis of public reactions to the Kent State University affair (which conjoined interview statements with comments taken from news reports and editorial pages), and Suppasarn and Adams's (1984) study of public attitudes toward television violence.

Q-samples of an altogether different sort are illustrated by Kinsey and Taylor's (1982) study of political cartoons, Wallenstein's (1976) and

Brown's (1979) research on viewer reactions to political propaganda posters, and Goldman's (1984) use of photographs from *Time* magazine. In yet another application, Brown (1972), in making a methodological point, had subjects rank-order—in terms of "importance to me"—a Q-sample inventory of human body segments (each part typed on a card). The resulting Q-factors showed that body shape, when drawn on the basis of subjective criteria, was humanoid in appearance but startlingly different from what an anatomically correct rendition would look like. Given the centrality of subjectivity to all aspects of human life, the possibilities for sampling Q-items is enormous, bounded only, as the above examples illustrate, by the researcher's imagination and by the nature of the problem under investigation.

Finally, several *"standardized" Q-samples* are available. These include Block's (1961) Adjective Q-set for Nonprofessional Sorters (personality assessment) and the Butler-Haigh (1954) Q-sample for psychotherapeutic counseling (Butler, 1972; Cartwright, 1972).

Design Principles in Q-Samples

Q-samples are always representations of communication contexts. As such, they do not include all communication possibilities; hence, questions may be raised about the process of selecting some items while excluding others. There are two basic techniques for choosing items, and these serve as our second way of distinguishing between Q-sample types. The first is based on *unstructured sampling,* in which items presumed to be relevant to the topic at hand are chosen without undue effort made to ensure coverage of all possible sub-issues. The unstructured sample, therefore, provides a reasonably accurate "survey" of positions taken or likely to be taken on a given issue. The risk with unstructured samples is that some issue components will be under- or oversampled and, consequently, that a bias of some kind will be incorporated inadvertently into the final Q-sample.

Structured samples are composed more systematically and seek to avoid weaknesses found in the other. They also promote theory testing by incorporating hypothetical considerations into the sample. The customary practice is to apply the design principles of factorial experimentation whereby Q-sample statements or items are assigned to (experimental) conditions designated and defined by the researcher. This application can be deductive or inductive. A *deductive design* is based on a priori hypothetical or theoretical considerations. *Inductive designs* emerge from

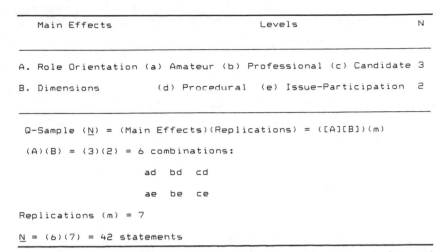

Main Effects	Levels	N
A. Role Orientation	(a) Amateur (b) Professional (c) Candidate	3
B. Dimensions	(d) Procedural (e) Issue-Participation	2

Q-Sample (N) = (Main Effects)(Replications) = ([A][B])(m)

(A)(B) = (3)(2) = 6 combinations:

                    ad   bd   cd

                    ae   be   ce

Replications (m) = 7

N = (6)(7) = 42 statements

Figure 2.1:   Factorial Design of Party Role Orientation Q-Sample (adapted from Carlson and Hyde, 1984).

the patterns that are observed as statements are collected. Furthermore, both types can incorporate few or many design conditions.

An example of a deductive factorial design is found in Carlson and Hyde's (1984) study of the impact of situations on role orientations of political party activists. Obtaining statements from published sources, they structured the items in a Q-sample conforming to the conditions, or "effects," displayed in Figure 2.1. Each role orientation (Amateur, Professional, Candidate) was reproduced along two dimensions (Procedural and Issue Participation) creating six possible combinations. Statements were assigned to each combination based on the authors' definitions of each category (such as Amateur Procedural [combination ad]: "Reforms that reduce the power of the party should be supported"). To allow for a variety of expressions, each combination was replicated seven times, producing a statement sample of 42 items. The empirical task was to discover whether and to what extent a sample of party activists displayed patterns of subjectivity consistent with such categorical distinctions.

Inductive designs differ only in the degree of theoretical elaboration that characterizes the sampling scheme. As an example, an inductive design was employed in the composition of the gay rights Q-sample, discussed earlier. The dimensions that guided the final assignment and selection of statements were suggested, for the most part, by the statements themselves and were not obvious prior to statement collection.

Q-Sorting and Conditions of Instruction

To reiterate, Q-sorting is a process whereby a subject models his or her point of view by rank-ordering Q-sample stimuli along a continuum defined by a condition of instruction. A *condition of instruction* is a guide for sorting Q-sample items. They can be *simple* requests for agreement and disagreement or *operationalizations of theoretical constructs.* Examples of the first type are as follows:

- Sort the items according to those with which you *most agree* (+5) to those with which you *most disagree* (–5).
- Sort the items according to those that are *most like* object/person X (+5) to those *most unlike* that object/person (–5).

In some cases, the same Q-sample is used with variations on the same basic condition of instruction. In a study of political perceptions, for example, a respondent could be asked to sort the sample items according to "what is most like/most unlike *your position,*" "what you believe is most like/most unlike a *conservative point of view,*" "what you believe is most like/most unlike a *liberal point of view,*" and so forth. In the Carlson and Hyde (1984) study of party role orientations, each subject used the same Q-sample items under three conditions of instruction, describing what he or she thought would be the characteristic point of view of a political *amateur,* a political *professional,* and a *candidate* running for public office.

Conditions of instruction also can be used to *operationalize hypothetical constructs and categories.* In this way theory testing occurs at the sorting stage. Referring again to the party-role orientations study (Carlson and Hyde, 1984), the amateur position was defined in the following scenario:

You are at a meeting composed of members of the League of Women Voters whose primary concern is increasing civic responsibility. You are invited to give a short speech. Use the statements in the Q-sort to indicate what themes you would most likely emphasize in your speech. Sort the statements from -4 (least likely to emphasize) to +4 (most likely to emphasize).

Carlson and Hyde then compared the results from this condition with the scenarios, that is, conditions of instruction, defining the professional and candidate perspectives. Multiple conditions of instruction such as these are especially useful in single case studies where the conditions can act as surrogates for behavioral hypotheses—that is, a respondent is asked to perform the Q-sort under different conditions because of the expectation that he or she will behave in a particular way. Whether or not a subject sees it the same way as the researcher is of course an empirical question: The validity of one's expectations or hypotheses is always tested against the Q-sorting behaviors of the subject. Hence the "utility" of a given condition of instruction depends upon the pattern of findings revealed in the factor structure.

Given this caveat, one can realize the research potential that conditions of instruction afford. In psychodynamic theory, for example, a central theoretical construct such as "superego" can be operationalized by the instruction "describe the type of person that your parents taught and wanted you to be." This deduction is based on the psychoanalytic understanding that the ego-ideal as a sub-branch of the superego is a psychic remnant of internalized parental expectations and values. Likewise, manifestations of the "id" might be stated: "Describe yourself as you are when you 'let down your hair,' set aside your inhibitions and act out your feelings" (see Ricks, 1972; Brown, 1974a, 1980, 1981).

Q-sorting procedures. When performing a Q-sort, a subject should have enough space to spread distribution markers from left to right of the middle 0 score (see Figure 2.2). A desk or card table is usually sufficient. Distribution markers are cards the same length as the statement cards (one for each + and − score and the 0 position in the middle) that reproduce the Q-sort continuum and assist the subject as he or she sorts the cards. Markers often contain an abridgement of the condition of instruction (for example, "most like my point of view" on the +5 marker and "most unlike my point of view" on the −5 marker), as well as the requested number of items in each segment of the continuum.

Positive scores are commonly placed, in ascending order, to the right of 0, and the negative ones to the left; it does not matter if they are reversed as long as all Q-sorts in the study are consistent.

(1) The subject(s) is asked to read through the items to become familiar with them. As this is done, the subject sorts them into three piles: Placed to the right are those with which the subject agrees, to the left those with which he or she disagrees, and in the middle those about which he or she is either neutral, ambivalent, or uncertain.

32

"MOST UNLIKE MY POINT-OF-VIEW"				NEUTRAL/NO SALIENCE				"MOST LIKE MY POINT-OF-VIEW"		
-5	-4	-3	-2	-1	0	+1	+2	+3	+4	+5
(3)	(4)	(4)	(7)	(7)	(10)	(7)	(7)	(4)	(4)	(3)
item	item	item	item	item	item	item	item	item	item	item
item	item	item	item	item	item	item	item	item	item	item
item	item	item	item	item	item	item	item	item	item	item
	item	item	item	item	item	item	item	item	item	
			item	item	item	item	item			
			item	item	item	item	item			
			item	item	item	item	item			
					item					
					item					
					item					

NAME (optional)_____ AGE_____ SEX ____Male

____Female

EDUCATION: ___High School ___Some College ___College ___College +

OCCUPATION:_____ RELIGIOUS AFFILATION:_____

PARTY ID.: ____ Republican ____ Democrat ____ Independent ____ Other

If you had opportunity to vote on "gay rights" protection laws, would you vote to repeal or not? ____ Repeal ____ Not Repeal ___?

Figure 2.2: Q-Sort Distribution and Score Sheet for Gay Rights Q-Study (*N* = 60 statement items).

(2) During Q-sorting, the subject spreads the items out under the distribution markers, while maintaining the general left-center-right relationships. This facilitates the reading of the items contextually and the making of comparisons.
(3) Studying the items to the right, and in conformity with the distribution, the subject selects the four items that are most like his

or her position (or, the number of items called for) and places them vertically, under the +5 marker (see Figure 2.2). The order of the items under the markers is not important; all four items beneath the +5 marker will receive the same score when the data are recorded.

(4) Turning now to the left side, the subject studies the items, and selects four from among those on the left that are most unlike his or her position. These are placed under the –5 marker. Again, the specific order does not matter.

(5) Returning to the right side, the subject now picks four items that are more like his or her position than the remaining ones among the grouping but which are not as significant as the four already selected (located under +5), and places them under the +4 marker. On second thought the respondent might decide that an item selected for + 4 is more important than one under +5. He or she is perfectly free to switch it with another at this or any other time.

(6) Attention reverts to the left side and the process is repeated, with the subject working toward the middle 0 position, until all of the Q-sort statements are positioned from left to right. Items placed under the middle marker (0) often are the ones left over after all of the positive and negative positions have been filled. The reason for having subjects work back and forth is to help them think anew the significance of each item in relation to the others. Once completed, the Q-sort should be reviewed, the subject making adjustments among items that, upon rearrangement, more accurately portray his or her personal point of view.

(7) Finally, statement scores for the completed Q-sort are recorded by writing the item numbers on a score sheet that reproduces the Q-sort distribution (see Figure 2.2). When the data are prepared for analysis, the statements for each rank are given the same value. Thus, in a continuum ranging from –5 to +5, each item under –5 would receive a 1, those under –4 would get a 2 and so forth to +5, which would be scored 11. One can also request additional demographic or other information by having the subjects respond to questions printed below the distribution of scores (Figure 2.2).

If another Q-sort (using the same Q-sample) is to be performed under a different condition of instruction, the cards should be regrouped, shuffled, and the previous steps repeated. Performing additional Q-sorts is less time-consuming since the subject is already familiar with the items and the sorting process. We recommend, however, that the subject not perform too many Q-sorts in rapid succession. For example, in an intensive single case study, in which the subject might describe 20 or more conditions of instruction, the Q-sorting should be spread out over several days.

Some Objections to Q-Sort Technique

Objections are sometimes raised about Q-technique procedures. In any study, the subject clearly is required to make many decisions regarding the salience, meaning, and relationship of each item to the others. An objection has been raised, for example, that the magnitude of the sorting task lies beyond the cognitive ability of most people to perform adequately (Bolland, 1985). Related is the criticism that the Q-sort continuum has too many categories and requires that subjects make too many and too fine distinctions among the items.

The "forced-free" distinction in Q-technique is also controversial. The Q-sort distribution is forced in that a certain number of items is prescribed for each rank; the subject is free, however, to place an item anywhere within the distribution. Finally, the practice of using an inverted quasi-normal distribution is believed to violate the principles of operant subjectivity.

The problems attributed to Q-technique are, in fact, more apparent than real when the method is put to actual use. Many technical conventions are utilitarian and not essential to the method's logic of inquiry. For example, within the forced distribution format, subjects retain complete freedom in placing the items. This is not unimportant, especially when compared to conventional ranking methods in which items are scored serially and contextual definition is thereby constrained. Although the range and the number of items permitted for each interval is predetermined the subject alone determines the meaning of the continuum. He or she also controls the specific rank and thus the contextual significance of each item. The prescribed distribution, therefore, is not an index of meaning, as in a scale; the index is entirely statistical so that, if all Q-sorts conform, their means and standard deviations are the same.[2]

Subjects frequently "violate" the format but neither the reliability of the technique nor the quality of the data are undermined by idiosyncratic sortings of the Q-sample. Both Brown (1971, 1985) and Cottle and McKeown (1980) demonstrate that the shape of a Q-sort distribution is methodologically and statistically inconsequential.

The recommended quasi-normal distribution is merely a device for encouraging subjects to consider the items more systematically than they otherwise might. In keeping with the Law of Error, it is assumed that fewer issues are of great importance than issues of less or no significance. Thus fewer items are found at the extremes. However, as Brown (1985) has said, it is only a convenience and not an empirical generalization.

The divisions along a Q-sort distribution can be mistaken for nominal rather than ordinal. They are not distinct categories wherein the items placed in a +3 position are cognitively and functionally separate from those put under +4. Instead, performing a Q-sort is a matter of ranking items on the basis of "more or less" rather than "either/or."

A question may be raised about the practice of having the distribution range from *most positive* to *most negative* rather than from most to least. An assumption of the latter option is that all responses contain some degree of the quality being defined; for example, "from most agree to least agree" implicitly asserts that everyone agrees to some extent. There is no option for no agreement or complete rejection. Q-technique, on the other hand, allows for both possibilities; a person can register agreement or disagreement by placing the Q-sample items on either side of the neutral point.

Furthermore, "most to least" assumes that the opposite of a concept is nothing more than the same thing, but to a lesser degree. Is the opposite of beautiful less beautiful? Might it not be ugliness, instead? Conservatives and liberals alike could argue that to be conservative is not just a matter of being less liberal but of holding to a point of view far different from the liberal ideology.

While performing a Q-sort, the subject draws distinctions on the basis of *psychological significance*. The poles of the opinion continuum thus represent a common unit of measurement in that items under +5 and -5 are assumed to hold "greater importance to me" than items elsewhere in the Q-sort. But what is of "greater importance to me" is *not* an artifact of an a priori designation by the researcher. It is a determination that only "I" (the sorter) can make by ranking at the poles those items that hold positive or negative salience vis-à-vis other items *in my opinion*. Hence, the middle score (0) is not an average but a point neutral in meaning and without psychological significance. All Q-sorts, therefore, are anchored in the same way, that is, at a point with no meaning where only the dispersion or variation of Q-sample items around it is dependent upon individual self-references (Stephenson, 1974).

3. PERSON SAMPLES AND THE SINGLE CASE

The concept of sampling has a twofold significance in Q methodology. In the first place, as we have noted, sampling principles and procedures are central to the design and composition of Q-samples. Whether such samples are constructed along structured or unstructured lines, the aim is always the same: to ensure a reasonably comprehensive and representative selection of a particular population of stimulus elements. We now turn to the issue of sampling in the second, more customary sense in which it is understood in behavioral research: the sampling of persons or respondent populations.

Most attention in Q methodology is given to statement samples (Q-samples); the person-sample (P-sample or P-set), however, is not unimportant. Because of its intensive orientation (Baas and Brown, 1973; Brown, 1974b; Lasswell, 1938), Q-method is biased toward small person-samples and single case studies, a preference in keeping with the behaviorist dictum that it is more informative to study one subject for 1,000 hours than 1,000 subjects for one hour (Skinner, 1969: 112). Q, in fact, is a method of and for the single case. This, we recognize, runs counter to conventional wisdom insofar as social scientists tend to regard the single case with suspicion. Single cases, as two political scientists have said, are "interesting and suggestive; but . . . do not provide the kind of general knowledge that will enable us to move from one situation to another and have some basis for predicting what we will see" (Hofferbert and Sharkansky, 1971: 1). It is not the purpose of Q-method to explore idiosyncrasy at the expense of general principles. Subjectivity and idiosyncrasy are not functional equivalents. Just as subjectivity is amenable to empirical analysis, so too can small P-sets and single case studies sustain meaningful generalizations about behavioral dynamics. The purpose is to study intensively the self-referent perspectives of particular individuals in order to understand the lawful nature of human behavior. Specific sampling principles and techniques important in mainstream behavioral research are not necessarily relevant to person sampling in Q given the contrasting research orientations and purposes. Subject selection, therefore, can be governed by *theoretical* (persons are chosen because of their special relevance to the goals of the study) or by *pragmatic* (anyone will suffice) considerations.

In this section, we discuss procedures for creating person-samples and for selecting "specimen" subjects for intensive analysis. From this discussion, the reader will become more aware of Q methodology as a strategy linking qualitative and quantitative analyses. We also take up the issues of "generalization" and "lawfulness," seeking in the process to illuminate the specific manner in which the philosophical, technical, and statistical components of Q methodology are conjoined.

Extensive and Intensive Person-Samples

The terms "extensive" and "intensive" are defined contextually. A survey of 50 subjects, for example, likely would be intensive according to R-based criteria but extensive in Q. Also, the nature of subjectivity under investigation is a factor. Typically, studies of "intersubjectivity," such as the homosexual rights example, are extensive because the intent is to determine the variety of views on an issue. Therefore, 50 to 100 people may perform Q-sorts with the same Q-sample under an identical condition of instruction. An intensive study, on the other hand, reflects interest in "intrasubjectivity," that is, in an in-depth examination of one person who sorts the Q-sample under many different conditions of instruction. Hence, what is small or large, single or many, intensive or extensive ultimately depends upon the nature and purpose of the study.

Extensive Person-Samples

The drawing of extensive person-samples is often affected by simple pragmatic considerations, namely, who is available? Subjects in the homosexual rights illustration, for example, were university faculty, staff, and students responding to a general appeal for research participants. No special effort was made to ensure complete representativeness across respondent characteristics (age, party identification, religion, etc.) since the purpose was to explore the attitudes in the population—a task obviously antecedent to ascertaining the numerical incidence and demographic correlates of such opinions.

Given the nonrandom nature of the gay rights person-sample, there is no claim that the three viewpoints exhaust the full range of attitudes toward homosexuality. If one suspects other perspectives exist, finding them is a simple matter of throwing the person-sample "net" wider. Nothing precludes adding more subjects to a respondent pool. Nevertheless, as Brown (1986) notes, the Q-factors that do emerge are themselves *generalizations of attitudes* held by persons defining a given factor. As such, they permit direct comparisons of attitudes as attitudes irrespective of the number of people who subscribe to them.

Mere availability, therefore, is one criterion for creating person-samples. Systematic criteria can be applied, however, and in this connection *factorial designs* are frequently employed in the same fashion that structured Q-samples are drawn. A factorially designed P-sample thus

Dimensions	Types			N
A. Sex	(a) Male	(b) Female		2
B. Age	(c) 20-40	(d) 41-60	(e) 61 and older	3
C. Education	(f) no college		(g) college	2
D. "Orientation"				
Group	(h) Mainline Protestant Churches			3
	(I) Evangelical-Fundamentalist Churches			
	(j) Gay/Lesbian Organizations			

P-Sample ($\underline{n}$) = (Criteria)(Replications) = ([A][B][C][D])(m)

(A)(B)(C)(D) = (2)(3)(2)(3) = 36 combinations

Replications (m) = 3

$\underline{n}$ = (36)(3) = 108 subjects for study

Figure 3.1:   Hypothetical Factorial Design for a Gay Rights Q-Study Person-Sample

marks an overt attempt to sample people of theoretical interest. It provides a degree of comprehensiveness not found in samples chosen solely on the basis of availability.

To illustrate, consider a possible replication of the gay rights study. Respondents could be selected according to criteria in some way linked to subjective viewpoints. For example, one might wish to compare the attitudes of gay rights activists with those of religiously active Protestant Christians. The latter can be distinguished further to compare "liberal" mainline denominations and "conservative" evangelical or fundamentalist branches. In addition, other demographic categories possibly related to the perspectives could be included (e.g., sex, level of education, age). These possibilities are represented in the factorial design shown in Figure 3.1. In this case, three persons replicate each combination for a total sample of 108 respondents.

Theoretical sampling. Other forms of purposive sampling (sometimes referred to as "dimensional" sampling; see Arnold, 1970) build theoretical considerations into the design. A variation on the gay rights P-set could model the "triple-appeal principle" presented by Lasswell (1932). Drawing upon psychoanalytic psychology, Lasswell contends that the personal meaning of objects follows from their relationship with one or more branches of the individual's psychic structure: impulse (id), conscience (superego), and reason (ego). A person responds to other people, institutions, symbols, policies, and so forth in light of the appeals of these to the respective personality components and the individual's dominant mode of psychological functioning. This principle has implications for the analysis of political communications. For instance, it could be applied to a study of the controversy surrounding homosexual rights based on the working hypothesis that these arguments would be accepted or rejected as a result of a person's "psychological strategy," that is, does he or she respond primarily on the basis of feeling, logic, or conscience, and/or a particular combination of them?

Pursuing this example, the triple appeal principle could be substituted for religion in the design ("Appeal" in place of "Orientation Group" for dimension D in Figure 3.1), with the total number of possible combinations remaining the same. Respondents representing *impulse* (type h) would be drawn from occupations and social positions where, for example, "bohemian" lifestyles prevail. Representatives of *reason* (type i) would be selected from among economic, scientific, and technological institutions, and those characteristic of *conscience* (type j) taken from institutions in which rectitude is fundamental (e.g., the clergy).

The use of factorial designs in P-set construction is subject to the same disclaimers accompanying their use in Q-sample composition. There is no assumption that all relevant population variables are included. Nor is it assumed that theoretical possibilities (e.g., Lasswell's hypothesis) governing respondent selection exhaust *all* possibilities or in any sense are "fully specified models" of the theory from which they are drawn.

In addition, P-set designs (and the theoretics and demographics they incorporate) can be used during data analysis and factor interpretation, especially when factors are rotated judgmentally. Assume again that Christians with particular denominational affiliations hold a hostile, contemptuous attitude toward homosexuals. Their religious understandings, in other words, lead them to a specific position on a particular social moral issue. This possibility can be given propositional footing and "tested" with a sufficiently well-structured P-set. If religious identification deserves credit as a prime mover on this issue, the data will be supportive: Factor saturations should be relatively dense and uniform for persons of that affiliation.[4] In the same spirit, P-set distinctions can be treated as "levels" in an experimental design, with religious affiliation the main effect to be analyzed via ANOVA of factor loadings. The use of P-sets in this fashion, however, is always subservient to the task of viewing things as the subject sees them.

Intensive Person-Samples

Intensive analysis is a logical extension of basic Q-methodological principles. The purpose of an intensive study is to explore the dynamics of intrapersonal subjectivity discovered in the extensive analysis. "Intensive" may mean an "*n* of 1" but is not limited to the single case; several people can be examined in detail.

There are systematic means for selecting individuals—"specimen" cases—for in-depth analysis. A *specimen,* in this connection, is an individual who is demonstrably "saturated with," and hence representative of, the kind of subjectivity one wishes to examine. The principles and procedures involved are now illustrated, by example, in three "steps."

Step 1—extensive phase: A group of respondents sort an identical Q-sample under a common condition of instruction. In an intensive analysis of the interpersonal worlds of persons of differing political orientation, Thomas (1979) had 53 respondents complete a "political ideology" Q-sample by rank-ordering N = 48 statements drawn from conventional scales designed to assess ideological position across the left-right spectrum. The 53 Q-sorts were correlated and factor analyzed. Four principal axis factors were rotated to a position of simple structure and factor scores were computed; factor arrays were examined to discern which factor was the most "radical" and which the most "conservative." Two factors were selected for further study. As it turned out, the second was more "moderately liberal" than conservative; the first, however, was clearly radical. (See Thomas, 1979, for presentation of factor scores substantiating these labels.)

Step 2—specimen selection: Individuals representing the points of view revealed in the extensive analysis are selected for intensive analysis. In principle, *any* person loaded on a factor is a candidate, since he or she "speaks the language" of the factor. However, some respondents are more representative of a given viewpoint than others. Hence the best candidates for intensive analysis are those whose factor loadings are the "purest" of all persons associated with that viewpoint. In the Thomas example, the six respondents with the highest loadings on each of the ideology factors were selected as specimen-representatives of the radical and moderate viewpoints. In this way subject selection is operant—dependent upon the subjects' own definitions—rather than intuitive or arbitrary.

Step 3—intensive analysis: Once a subject (or subjects) has been selected, probes appropriate to the study are administered. An intensive analysis is ripe for multivariate-multimethod approaches. Additional Q-sorts may be given, including the original Q-sample used in the extensive stage but now sorted under new conditions of instruction. Different Q-samples and instructions can be employed as well. Conventional scales and tests may be relevant; frequently, these are used to interpret or rethink the Q-sort findings.

In the Thomas study, each of the 12 participants in the intensive phase of the study discussed, autobiographically, past and present interpersonal relationships important in his or her life. From these accounts, a sample of "significant others" for each subject was drawn. Added to these were a variety of self-conceptions and political figures and symbols salient to American politics during the 1970s. Each person then described each of the self-conceptions, primary-interpersonal, and secondary-political objects with the Anderson (1968) "likability" Q-sample referred to in Section 2. In all, each subject described some 30 objects, thus performing 30 separate operations with the same Q-sample.

Data analysis was conducted intraindividually, resulting in a Q-factor analytic model of the personal-political object-world of each respondent. In these cases, factors represented categories of objects described similarly by the respondent. At issue, among other things, was the relationship between the primary and secondary objects of perception. If, as Lasswell (1930) suggested, an intrapsychic connection exists between the primary and secondary and we respond to the latter in terms of the former, we would anticipate evidence to this effect to emerge in the factor structures. Put negatively, we would *not* expect to find factors defined solely by political objects. Rather, political objects should *share* factor space with primary self-other objects, and this was found to be the case. The specific alignment of primary and secondary objects varied from person to person, but such particularities are only idiosyncratic variations on the general, dynamic principle whereby primary-object constellations serve, consciously or not, as perceptual prisms through which one's experience of the more remote political object-world is structured or given order (Lasswell, 1930).

An Exemplification

Space precludes a complete recapitulation, but brief reference to one of the more noteworthy findings from these case studies may be instructive in pointing to the theoretical value of intensive analysis. In the spirit of exemplification, Figure 3.2 presents a graphic depiction of a portion of the factor matrices of two "key informants" from the Thomas (1979) research. Of particular interest in this regard is the distinguishing manner in which the radical "Jim" and the moderate "Kathy" have described "good" and "bad" objects from the respective primary-political object-worlds. The objects in this case are actually Q-sort descriptions, and their location in two-factor space is produced by simply plotting the respective loadings of each variate on each of a pair of politically relevant factors extracted from the Q-sort data supplied by each individually.

The selection of these cases for demonstration is not arbitrary. On the contrary, it is governed by theoretical sampling (Glazer and Strauss, 1967) inasmuch as the political ideology Q-sorts provided by Jim and Kathy had the highest loadings of any of the respondents on each of the radical and moderate factors taken from the initial, extensive phase of the study. This fact holds important implications for the intensive analysis wherein an attempt was made to interrogate the possible psychogenesis of the contrasting political convictions displayed by radical and moderate ideologues. Research of this kind was quite common during the 1960s and 1970s, when a vast social science literature was accumulating on questions pertaining to the psychological character, correlates, and genesis of New Left world views (Keniston, 1973).

When such accounts sought to probe beneath the demographic correlates of New Left radicalism and inquire into interpersonal and intrapsychic dynamics, researchers were forced to abandon large numbers and focus instead, in an in-depth, clinical fashion, on a handful of key informants. As a consequence of altering the observational standpoint, investigators were able to generate several intriguing hypotheses as to why certain personalities and certain background experiences seemed to be more congenial than others to New Left ideological appeals. In the process, however, authors of clinical case histories inevitably encountered the Achilles heel of such approaches on the question of generalization. Keniston (1968), for example, in one of the more thoughtful ventures of this kind, an intensive study of activist leaders of the "Vietnam Summer" project, lamented, after completing his interviews, that "I am still not sure

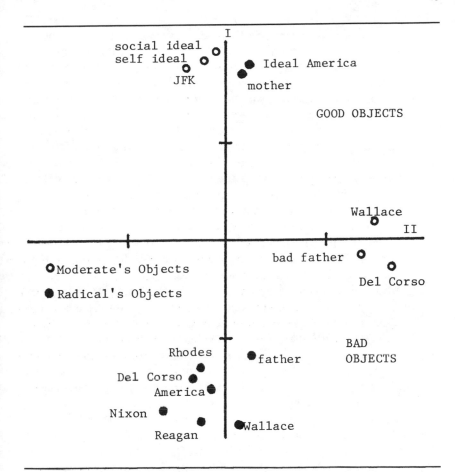

Figure 3.2: Factorial Relationship of Good and Bad Objects for Moderate and Radical Subjects (adapted from Thomas, 1979).

how one would go about finding a 'typical' group of radicals" (p. 19). With the specimen selection technology afforded by Q-method's approach to intensive analysis, this uncertainty can be reduced substantially, if not obviated entirely.

Among several speculations spawned by the case history accounts of student radicalism, one of the more intriguing centered on the possible idcological implications of differential identification with parents on the part of young radicals, especially males, in comparison with their more conservative or moderate cohorts. Specifically, life history interviews were leading researchers to portray young radical males as "mother identified," a tendency that was subject to interpretation in one of two, not altogether distinct, ways. In what we can call the "minimalist" account, male radicalism was regarded as having at least part of its roots in a rather strong identification with the mother, which (in turn) led to an empathic capacity for "nurturant identification" (Keniston, 1968) with society's downtrodden and dispossessed. The "maximalist" view, on the other hand, took its cues from classical psychoanalytic theory and embraced an all-out "Oedipal rebellion" interpretation of the young radical male (e.g., Marmor, 1968; Meissner, 1974). Though moribund at present, the New Left and the extent to which its psychic roots can be fairly portrayed in either of such accounts are still issues of debate among social scientists (see Rothman and Lichter, 1982). But what matters in this connection is what Q methodology can provide by way of the sort of compelling public demonstration of evidence that is absent from impressions gleaned on the basis of life history interviews, no matter how carefully conducted.

On this score, the data displayed in Figure 3.2 are illustrative of the kinds of complex, intricate psychodynamics that interview data suggest but cannot demonstrate. Noteworthy are two features of the objects-worlds of Jim and Kathy. First, the radical Jim splits good and bad objects into mutually exclusive (mirror image) categories at opposite ends of one bipolar factor. Moderate Kathy, on the other hand, portrays good and bad in more muted, orthogonal-factor terms. This structural alignment of good and bad held equally well for the other specimens of radical and moderate views. Second, and more to the point of parental identification, Jim's bipolar factor gives eloquent testimony to the political significance of a "special closeness to mother" coupled with a severely impaired identification with father. At the positive end of Jim's Q-sort description of how he would have liked America to be ideally, one finds also his description of his mother. On the negative side of this factor are his descriptions of then-president Nixon, Spiro Agnew, and Ronald Reagan, all of whom are ascribed the same negative qualities Jim resented in his father. These same Oedipal-like patterns show up in the factor structures of other radical specimens, and they are corroborated as well by additional non Q-sort data too complex to summarize here. They do not appear in Kathy's data—the only primary "bad object" on her second factor is her description of how she recalled her father ("mad father") when she was particularly angry with him—nor do they show up in the factor structures of the remaining moderate specimens. Data such as these will in no way sustain an effort to generalize to all persons of a particular ideological stripe. What they will sustain, however, is the development of generalizations with applicability of a particular "known quantity," in this case the "Oedipal radical" as hinted at in the clinical literature but brought into operational form via the Q-methodological approach to intensive analysis. The numerical preponderance or relative distribution of such types in a larger population, radical or otherwise, is an issue that intensive analysis is neither suited nor intended to address.

Science and the Single Case

The major concern of Q methodology is not with how many people believe such-and-such, but with why and how they believe what they do. Thus the central issue is from what perspective can relationships best be observed? All else is secondary to observational perspectives.

As we have indicated, the perspective is external in R-based research. Specific person-sampling procedures are necessary because of the initial uncertainty on the part of the researcher that he or she correctly understands the respondents' frames of reference. It is thus axiomatic in conventional attitude research that validity and reliability tests are essential since the researcher's external perspective operantly expressed in scale construction must be tested against the subjects' perspectives. Accordingly, the use of large respondent samples is in order to control for measurement error. In Q methodology, on the other hand, small numbers of respondents, including single cases, are psychometrically acceptable since the observational perspective is the respondent's own. Any interpretive accounts advanced by researchers, then, are subservient to the respondent's frame of reference as made operant by Q-sorting. It is for this reason that the validity and reliability tests so central to conventional scaling in mainstream attitude research are simply unessential within the psychometric framework of Q methodology.

Finally, we need to reconsider the notion that single case studies, no matter how intriguing, are inherently suspect and of limited value. Such a view stems partly from linguistic confusion. Since examination of single cases has come to mean literally the study of *one* person, group, country, and so forth, the terms "individual" and "case" are often used interchangeably. But as Lundberg (1941) has pointed out, this association is merely a verbal convention. Strictly speaking, cases so conceived are *not* at issue in scientific investigation. "What science actually deals with are events, occurrences, and instances—i.e., with discovery and prediction from behavioral units" (Brown, 1974b: 4). There is no reason to argue that the study of such events cannot take place within the confines of one person's "behavioral universe" (Stephenson, 1985). The criticism that one is trying to generalize or predict from a single case simply because the instances are an individual's behaviors is "just another of those misconceptions due to ambiguous language and lack of rigorous, operational, analytical thinking" (Lundberg, 1941: 380).

When we reconceptualize "case" to refer to a behavioral event, we also view the individual person as a complex *configuration of events*. This understanding makes it possible to inquire into the lawful regularities among such events and draw conclusions not unlike the generalizations derived from extensive, cross-sectional comparisons of many individuals in terms of some trait or set of traits. Hence, the basic *law of Q methodology* is the "transformation of subjective events into operant factor structure" (Stephenson, 1970-1980: 205). Consequently, we agree with Hofferbert and Sharkansky (1971): Single cases are interesting and suggestive; but more than that, they advance general knowledge about the process by which subjective worlds are constructed and experienced.

4. STATISTICAL ANALYSIS

Data analysis in Q methodology typically involves the sequential application of three sets of statistical procedures: correlation, factor analysis, and the computation of factor scores. In light of its sophistication and broader methodological centrality, factor analysis and its application are matters that warrant particular attention. For reasons of space and purpose, our discussion is intentionally brief, stressing the conceptual and practical aspects of statistical method. Readers may wish to pursue technical and computational aspects as presented in detail by Brown (1980).

Q vs. R Factor Analysis

Preliminary to a consideration of factor analysis, it is essential to clarify what is in fact being factored. As most readers are no doubt already aware, the psychometrics of Q call for the correlation and factoring of persons as opposed to tests, traits, and the like (R-method). This distinction, although accurate, is insufficient since misconceptions continue to abound on what

TABLE 4.1
Raw Data Matrix

		A	B	C	. . .	N
				T r a i t s		
P	a	$_aX_A$	$_aX_B$	$_aX_C$	. . .	$_aX_N$
e	b	$_bX_A$	$_bX_B$	$_bX_C$	. . .	$_bX_N$
r	c	$_cX_A$	$_cX_B$	$_cX_C$	. . .	$_cX_N$
s	.	,	,	,	,	,
o	.	,	,	,	,	,
n	.	,	,	,	,	,
s	n	$_nX_A$	$_nX_B$	$_nX_C$	,	$_nX_N$

SOURCE: Adapted from Brown (1980).

is meant. Technically, the persons versus traits distinction has led some (e.g., Russett, 1971; Rummel, 1970; Nie et al., 1975) to infer, erroneously, that Q-method is fundamentally and merely "inverted" Q-factor analysis: that it is really nothing more than the application of R-method factoring technique to a transposed data matrix in which "cases of observation" and "measures" of those cases are exchanged for one another for purposes of analysis.

The connection between Q and R can be made with reference to the relationships shown in a simple raw data matrix (Table 4.1) in which the scores of n persons on N traits are shown. In R-method, correlation summarizes the relationships among, and factor analysis denotes the clusters of, the N traits. What is important in this connection is that the units of measurement for the N traits are singly centered by column. Trait A, for example, will be regarded as a measure of intelligence; hence all values in column A are expressed in terms of IQ scores. Depending on its nature, trait B may be measured in terms of some other unit (e.g., daily caloric intake). In the course of correlating A with B, a normalization of the statistical distribution within each column is effected as a function of Pearson's expression $r_{A, B} = (\Sigma z_A z_B)/n$, where n is the number of persons in the sample. Correlational analysis results in an $N \times N$ matrix and factor analysis will produce a matrix $m \times N$, where m indicates the number of underlying dimensions on which the N traits cluster together.

To appreciate that Q is altogether different from "inverted" factor analysis, we need to consider what it would mean to transpose this data matrix (which is precisely what would be done if an investigator were interested in searching out, via correlational and factor analysis, the m clusters of people on the N traits). In the transposed matrix, columns would be people and rows the measurements on N traits. In this procedure, columns now consist of scores the statistical distributions of which are no longer singly centered around a common unit of measurement. The first two entries in column A are now expressed in terms of the first subject's intelligence quotient and daily caloric consumption. As a practical matter, there is nothing to prevent correlating persons (columns) in this fashion, but what possible meaning could be attributed to the deviation of mean scores (effected by the normalization subsumed in correlation) when they are composed of such diverse measuring units? "At a minimum," as Brown (1980: 15) notes, "correlation and factor work assumes linearity, and it is this linearity that is missing . . . when the measuring units differ." What sense does it make to say that an IQ score of 140 (trait A) has "lesser value" than 3,000 calories a day (trait B) when such scores are expressed in such incommensurate units of measurement?

It did not take long for early practitioners of Q-factor analysis (which predated Q methodology) to recognize this problem. Once it was recognized and appreciated, it was not long until the inverted factoring technique had few proponents or psychometric promises to recommend it. And so it remained until Stephenson placed the "factoring of persons" on a more secure psychometric foundation by proposing a way out of the "units of measurement" cul de sac: *All observations in Q-technique are premised on a common unit of measurement, namely, "self-significance."* The "traits" composing a genuine Q-data matrix are singly centered around a mean of psychological significance, that is, "importance to me." An "exceptional" IQ may or may not now hold lesser value than an "average" number of daily calories. Although the prospect of having to distinguish between such items within one's "universe of importance" is a bit unsavory, if not absurd, it demonstrates the principle: Statements to the effect that A > B or vice versa now have meaning for measurement purposes; hence, the assumption of linearity is satisfied. Consequently, correlation and factor analysis are practicable. At issue in the difference between Q and R is something much more than the application of the same factoring technique to the identical, albeit "upside down," data matrix. Indeed, as Stephenson (1953b: 15) has emphatically stated, "there never was a single matrix of scores to which both Q and R apply."

Factor Analysis: Principles and Purposes in Q

Factor analysis is fundamental to Q methodology since it comprises the statistical means by which subjects are grouped—or, more accurately, group themselves—through the process of Q-sorting. One point should be clear: "Q-factor analysis" does not constitute a distinct set of statistical procedures for identifying like-minded persons (or similarly arranged Q-sorts) in the same sense that centroid and principle components are differing methods for extracting factors. Once Q-sorts have been collected and correlated, the mathematics of the factoring process are virtually identical to those followed in R-method applications. In fact, it is in statistical respects that Q and R are most alike, despite the persistent (and mistaken) notion that they somehow represent rival factor analytic systems. When practitioners of Q and R quibble over statistical specificities (e.g., how to determine a factor's significance, rotation, and the like) their differences derive from deeper methodological considerations, not from any technical particularities per se. It is in this light, for instance, that Stephenson's preference for the centroid method over alternative factoring techniques is best understood. The first method to be elaborated in factoring theory, the centroid or *simple summation method* (Burt, 1940), was distinguished by its computational ease compared to more elegant and mathematically precise factoring systems (principal components) that followed. Stephenson's continued use of the earlier method well into the computer age, however, is not due to computational convenience but stems from theoretical considerations, as noted below.

As a practical matter, the factoring process commences once a matrix of Q-sort correlations is provided. It makes virtually no difference, as Brown (1971) has shown, whether the coefficients in the correlation matrix are Pearson's *r*, Spearman's *rho,* or any other commonly employed non-parametric measure of association. Likewise, it makes little difference whether the specific factoring routine is the principal components, centroid, or any other available method. Regardless of the precise procedures employed, the resultant factor structures differ little from one another in any appreciable respects (Burt, 1972). Our concern here is with the *principles* and *products* of factor analysis as applied in Q-studies, not with the statistical *means* by which these principles are effected or these products realized. The latter issues subsume mathematical complexities extending well beyond the scope of this monograph. They are discussed at considerable length in volumes by Adcock (1954), Harman (1976), Rummel (1970), and Brown (1980: Part II—Technical Procedures) and in monographs in the QASS series by Kim and Mueller (1978a, 1978b).

TABLE 4.2
Correlations as Related to Factor Loadings

Subjects	Correlations					Factor Loadings			Factor Weights
	1	2	3	4	5	A	B	C	
1		.61	.62	.63	.59	.80	.08	.02	2.22
2			.61	.60	.54	.79	.05	-.07	2.08
3				.56	.70	.77	-.07	-.13	1.88
4					.68	.76	-.06	.16	1.77
5						.75	.14	.24	1.70

What is *accomplished* by factor analysis, however, is worthy of attention, and this can be illustrated with reference to the minimatrix in Table 4.2. This matrix presents the Pearsonian correlations among the five Q-sorts defining Factor A in the gay rights study discussed earlier. Also shown are the loadings of these subjects on each of the three principal components factors extracted from the complete correlation matrix. The correlation coefficients are uniformly high, indicating that the statements in the Q-sample in fact were arranged similarly by these five persons. However, the sheer size of the matrix, housing $n(n-1)/2$ relationships in all, is a formidable obstacle to discerning the patterns readily disclosed by factor analysis. All that the factor analysis does is lend statistical clarity to the behavioral order implicit in the matrix by virtue of similarly (or dissimilarly) performed Q-sorts. Factorization simplifies the interpretive task substantially, bringing to attention the typological nature of audience segments on any given subjective issue.

Factor loadings are in effect correlation coefficients: They indicate the extent to which each Q-sort is similar or dissimilar to the composite *factor array* (model Q-sort, discussed below) for that type. The standard error for a zero-order factor loading is given by the expression SE = $1/\sqrt{N}$, where N = the number of items in the Q-sample. Since the gay rights Q-sample contained 60 items, the standard error of factor loadings displayed in Table 1.1 is SE = $1/\sqrt{60}$ = .129. Loadings in excess of 2.58 (SE) = + / –.33 are therefore statistically significant at the .01 level, and these are indicated by italics in Table 1.1.

Theoretical vs. Statistical Significance of Factors

The procedure for determining whether or not a *factor* (as opposed to a *loading* on a factor) is "significant" is not as straightforward: A variety of statistical criteria and, alternatively, theoretical criteria can be employed in making that determination. Of the statistical options, the most common practice is to employ the *eigenvalue* criterion, whereby a factor's significance (importance) is estimated by the sum of its squared factor loadings. (Eigenvalues divided by the number of variates—Q-sorts in Q, traits in R—equals the percentage of the total variance accounted for by a factor.) By convention, factors with eigenvalues greater than 1.00 are considered significant; those with eigenvalues of lesser magnitude are considered too weak to warrant serious attention.

Caution should be exercised when such purely statistical criteria are used. First, factors may be produced that are statistically significant but substantively without meaning. It is quite possible to extract a factor whose eigenvalue is greater than 1.00, but on which the loadings of all respondents do not exceed the standard error of a zero-order loading, the criterion of significance in this case being an artifact of Q-sample and P-set size (Brown, 1980: 42-43). Second, the sole imposition of statistical criteria may lead one to overlook a factor that, although unimportant in terms of the proportion of the variance explained, nevertheless may hold special theoretical interest. This is illustrated by Brown (1980) in terms of a Q-study of decision making in a psychiatric hospital where four factors were found, each indicative of a different perspective among ward team members. By the eigenvalue criterion, however, only three factors would have been extracted. The fourth factor's statistical weakness was revealed in the marginal loadings of all but one respondent. In this case, though, the $n = 1$ respondent was the ward physician, that is, the one person on the team who held ultimate decision-making authority and whose viewpoint, no matter how unpopular, usually carried the day. "Consequently, the importance of a factor cannot be determined by statistical criteria alone, but must take into account the social and political setting to which the factor is organically connected" (Brown, 1980: 42; also see Brown, 1979). In sum, it is important to distinguish between the theoretical and the statistical significance of factors in Q methodology. As a general principle, Q emphasizes the former while foregoing sole reliance on the latter. At a practical level, common sense offers the best counsel when determining the importance of factors, that is, their contextual significance in light of the problems, purposes, and theoretical issues in the research project.

Rotating to a Terminal Solution

The distinction between theoretical and statistical significance surfaces again on the issue of factor rotation. What the "objective" rotational schemes (*varimax, quartimax, equimax*) share is the statistical quest for simple structure. Of the various mathematical methods by which *simple structure* can be approximated, the varimax method of orthogonal rotation is probably the most frequently employed; this is true of Q-studies as well. The purpose is to maximize the purity of saturation of as many variates (Q-sorts) as possible on one or the other of the *m* factors extracted initially. Simple structure enhances orthogonality if the data sustain it—since, in the optimum case, Q-sorts will have high loadings on one factor with near-zero loadings on the other(s). Simple structure enhances interpretation insofar as factor-types bear a fairly direct correspondence to "known quantities"—that is, actual Q-sorts or traits in R—with the amount of "muddling" due to mixed and null cases being held to a minimum.

Following much the same logic used to distinguish between theoretical and statistical significance of factors, Q methodologists eschew strictly mathematical criteria in favor of the theoretical, judgmental rotation of factors (Stephenson, 1953b; Brown, 1980). Depending on the problem, there may be good reasons to abandon simple structure for "simplest structure" (Stephenson, 1953b; Thompson, 1962). In the subsequent chapter we illustrate judgmental rotation in greater detail. Generally, however, its practicality is indicated on those occasions where a particular Q-sort (e.g., the ward physician mentioned earlier) holds special interest, although, in the wake of varimax rotation, it may be a mixed case in the overall factor matrix. Thus it can prove theoretically advantageous to treat that Q-sort as a *reference variate* and proceed with judgmental rotation to maximize its loading on one factor. In the process the loadings of other Q-sorts will change—some former pure types becoming mixed and vice versa—but the underlying relationships, summarized in the correlation matrix, will not. What rotation effects is a change in the *vantage point* from which data are viewed. In the hospital study, the decision making perspectives of ward team members are judged in light of their relationship to the authoritative source of those decisions.

For these reasons, the centroid method, widely dismissed because of its indeterminacy (there is no mathematically correct solution out of the infinite number possible), is still the factoring method of choice for Stephenson. Having no correct solution, it frees one to follow hunches (abductive logic) and to approach problems from any number of different angles that theory might recommend.

Factor Scores

In most research applications, factor interpretation proceeds on the basis of factor loadings. In Q, on the other hand, interpretations are based primarily on the factor scores. Once again, space prohibits attention to computational details (Creaser, 1955; Brown, 1980), but the general procedure can be summarized. The task is to generate a *factor array* or model Q-sort—one for each factor—with scores ranging from +5 to –5 (if these were the values anchoring the positive and negative ends of the opinion continuum when the Q-sorts were administered). The recommended procedure for computing factor scores is to designate as defining variates only those Q-sorts that are solely and significantly loaded on a given factor and to merge them in computing an array for that type. As differences in the magnitude of significant loadings indicate, however, some Q-sorts are more closely associated with the viewpoint of a particular factor than are others. Accordingly, the mechanics of factor scoring call first for the calculation of factor weights whereby these differing magnitudes are taken into account. The relevant expression is given by Spearman (1927) as:

$$w = \frac{f}{1-f^{e}}$$

where f is the factor loading and w its weight. In the case of respondent 1 in the example above (Table 4.2), $f = .80$ and the resulting weight is 2.22, whereas the weight for respondent 5 is only 1.70. Consequently, 1's Q-sort will count 1.3 times as much as 5's in calculating scores for factor A. Factor scores are computed as *z-scores,* but for convenience are converted into whole numbers (+5 to –5) to facilitate comparisons between factor arrays. Finally, these scores can be compared to determine that Q-sample items are distinguishing, that is, placed in significantly different locations in the opinion continuum for any two factors. To do this it is necessary to estimate the respective errors of the scores and to incorporate these into the formula for determining the *standard error of the difference:*

$$SED_{x-y} = \sqrt{SE_x^2 + SE_y^2}$$

where x and y represent scores given the same statement by factors x and y, and SE refers to the *standard error* for each of these scores. The latter, in turn, is given by the expression:

$$SE_{fm} = s_x \sqrt{1 - r_{xx}}$$

where S_x is the standard deviation of the forced Q-sort distribution, r_{xx} a factor's reliability, and SE_{fs} the standard error of the factor scores. Thus the issue of reliability is implicated in determining whether factor scores are significantly different between factors. Indeed, its effect here is such that the magnitude of error associated with factor scores diminishes as factor reliability increases. Therefore, we must estimate a factor's reliability before identifying distinguishing items. Assuming that the same person will render Q-sort orderings with the same Q-sample at different times that correlate upwards of .80, a factor's reliability can be estimated using the expression:

$$r_{xx} = \frac{0.80p}{1 + (p - 1)0.80}$$

where p is the number of persons defining a factor and .80 the estimated reliability coefficient. Once distinguishing statements are determined, it is possible to interpret the factors contextually—a process illustrated in our final chapter.

5. RESEARCH APPLICATIONS

The range of applications in Q methodology is enormous, spanning hundreds of different problems across the spectrum of the social and behavioral sciences (see, e.g., Brown, 1968). Though a virtue, this versatility counsels prudence in any attempt to "walk through" a "typical" Q-study. Nevertheless, the narrowly technical and broader methodological issues involved are best presented in actual case studies.

In this section we illustrate two applications of Q methodology, each approached in a manner appropriate to the particular task at hand. We repeat a previous point: Though premised on common principles—especially self-referentiality as it relates to subjectivity—Q-studies may vary considerably in their design and execution yet be "sound" methodologically.

Study 1. The Elusive Concept of Civil Religion

Few topics rival politics and religion in their capacity to ignite individual passions and inflame public controversy. When conversations once confined to one realm spill over into the other, the result is indeed a highly combustible state of affairs. The contemporary debate in American politics instigated by the politicization of Christian fundamentalism illustrates this relationship; yet it is but one chapter in a dialogue of centuries-old duration. The modern terms of that dialogue were established initially by Rousseau in connection with the concept of "civil religion." For Rousseau, civil religion had a distinct legitimating function made necessary by the impact of modernity on traditional notions of community, authority, and status (Nisbet, 1953).

The subject of sporadic attention in the interim, the concept of civil religion has been resurrected recently by sociologist Robert Bellah (1967), who defines it in terms of the political liturgies and symbols that serve as "a genuine vehicle of national religious self-understanding" (p. 29). The literature spawned by Bellah's essay shows remarkable continuity with earlier themes, particularly the role of civil religion in "symbolic legitimation" (Hughes, 1980). Thus, in the American context, civil religion has been credited with "civilizing the savage beast of the state," establishing freedom and order, and contributing to systemic stability (Linder and Pierard, 1978). Allegations of function and normative value, however, are predicated on premises as to the roles and meanings that civil religion may assume for the average person. Surely one can assert that civil religion symbolizes an "ultimate order of existence in which republican values and virtues make sense" (Bellah and Hammond, 1980: 12). To do so, however, in the absence of any empirical evidence as to how and why this may be the case, hardly qualifies as sound scientific practice.

One of the most interesting and certainly the most lamentable aspect of the civil religion literature is that it has been constructed on ambiguous, even tenuous, conceptual footings; this ambiguity is in part implicated in the debate over civil religion's normative consequences. The general tenor of Bellah's (1967) essay, for example, is sympathetic and affirmational toward civil religion. At the same time, he allows that it has been used as a subterfuge for special interests, unjust treatment of minorities, and justification for imperialistic foreign policy.

Explicating the various dimensions of civil religion, Martin Marty (1974) posits two major categories (two relationships between God and State): (1) the idea that *nation is dependent upon and under God's care and judgment,* and (2) the view that *minimizes God's involvement* by *stressing the self-transcendence of the state.* Both of these, furthermore, can be depicted in a mode that is either: (a) *priestly,* which will "normally be celebrative, affirmative, culture building" or (b) *prophetic,* which has a predisposition toward the judgmental. "[The first] comforts the afflicted; the other afflicts the comfortable" (Marty, 1974: 145).

Marty generates a 2 × 2 matrix whereby the modes and styles interact, yielding "two kinds of two kinds" of civil religion:

(1a) *Nation-Under-God: Priestly.* The deity provides the nation with identity, meaning, and purpose but exists "prior to and independently of the state and may be expected to outlive and outlast civil society."

(1b) *Nation-Under-God: Prophetic.* God both shapes and judges the nation; transcendence is expressed in terms of creation and justice.

(2a) *Nation-as-Transcendent: Priestly.* The deity's influence and power are transferred to the nation; emphasis is placed on the "promise of America" rather than the "promise to America."

(2b) *Nation-as-Transcendent: Prophetic.* The universal community of all nations (political ecumenicism) is proclaimed, as is self-determination without self-worship.

A virtue of this scheme is that it clarifies the possible patterns and permutations of civil religion while preparing the way for the normative debate. For the most part, evaluative discussions of civil religion have characterized as unwholesome the alleged tendency to move from the prophetic to the priestly mode (Linder and Pierard, 1978). To the extent, however, that American civil religion approximates Marty's "Nation-

Under-God: Prophetic" category, scholars have generally seen less cause for concern (see, e.g., Mead, 1975).

Civil religion in empirical research. Research on civil religion has focused in particular on questions of forms and effects. At issue in the former case is the "construct validity" of civil religion; that is, whether conceptual and theoretical typologies have any affinities with actual politico-religious beliefs. Results from initial research by Wimberley (1976; Wimberley et al., 1976) at first blush suggest an affirmative answer inasmuch as responses to a civil religion scale were highly interrelated. When the scale items themselves are inspected, however, it is not difficult to see why: They all partake of a particular—in this case, quite conservative— orientation toward the relationship of religion to politics. Missing is anything approximating the prophetic modes. Consequently, it is hard to disagree with Wimberley (1976: 350) that "civil religion seems to be a conservative orientation by definition." Given the operationalization of the concept, contrary findings were precluded at the outset. There is plenty to take issue with in this approach, or at least enough to cast doubt on Wimberley's (1976) conclusion that the concept of "civil religion" has achieved "scientific status."

Research on the *behavioral effects* of civil religion has been meager. Attention has been confined to studies of socialization and the effects of civil religious orientations on candidate choice (Smidt, 1980; Wimberley, 1980). If nothing else, the findings and the research strategies from which they derive stand as an instructive counterpoint to the application of Q methodology in addressing the concept of civil religion.

Q Methodology and the Concept of Civil Religion

The civil religion concourse. The literature on civil religion and recent debate on the role of religion in politics provide a rich "concourse of communication" (Stephenson, 1978b, 1986) vis-à-vis the concept of civil religion. Sampling from this concourse, statements were drawn from a variety of sources (e.g., interviews, speeches, historical documents, church publications, and letters to the editor). The final 60-item Q-sample does not incorporate a strict factorial design but contains two major components: Hence 22 statements relate to the general concept of civil religion, taking into account the priestly versus prophetic distinction, and 38 statements treat contemporary issues, particularly pro and con positions on the Moral Majority.

For purposes of comparison, data were collected at two different times in two separate locations. The study was conducted in Iowa ($n = 91$) during the 1980 presidential election campaign and in the state of Washington ($n = 53$) in January and February 1985. Although both data sets were drawn from respondents with Christian orientations, those in the Washington sample were identified with an evangelical and fundamentalist subculture.

In addition to the Q-sort, respondents completed a questionnaire soliciting information concerning political ideology, party identification, church affiliation, and views on various issues, persons, and organizations. The Washington version updated the original by incorporating questions about the 1984 presidential election; it also included a religiosity scale not used in the Iowa study. They were alike in all other respects.

In completing the Q-sorts, respondents followed the same forced distribution scheme for an $N = 60$ item Q-sample used in the gay rights study. The 91×91 Iowa correlation matrix was factor analyzed, using the principal components method with a varimax rotation. Several solutions were considered, but in this instance, as in the Washington case, a three-factor solution was deemed most adequate. Criteria for "adequacy" can vary from study to study, but in this case it was strongly indicated by the fact that 84 of the 91 Iowa subjects had loadings exceeding statistical significance on one or more of the three factors.

Comparing two-sample factor structures. Before turning to the factor scores and the task of interpretation, it is instructive to note how the initial three-factor solution derived from the Iowa data compares with the independently derived three-factor solution from Washington. In the latter case, 50 of the 53 respondents loaded significantly on at least one factor; as we shall see, there is substantial correspondence between the two solutions. To be sure, differences can be detected, but the variations, revealed in the factor scores, reflect nuances of meaning apparently deriving from the specific subcultures from which the respondent pools were drawn.

Evidence of between-sample comparability is found in Table 5.1, which reports correlations among the two sets of factor arrays. Of paramount interest are the coefficient entries in the diagonal. Thus Iowa:1 correlates with Washington:1, and the same match is true for factors 2 and 3. (Washington:3 also correlates with Iowa:1 and 2, a finding accounted for more fully in the complete report [McKeown and Thomas, 1985].)

The symmetry of the two factor structures is further confirmed when the six factor arrays from the two studies combined are subjected to a second-order Q-factor analysis. Displayed in Table 5.2, the resulting factor matrix indicates that, although the Iowa factors are somewhat less orthogonal than the Washington factors, the overall correspondence between the two

TABLE 5.1
Person-Sample/Factor Correlations

		Washington Sample		
		1	2	3
	1	.57*	−.36*	.49*
Iowa	2	.35*	.62*	.56*
Sample	3	.16	−.27	.56*

*Significant p < .01

TABLE 5.2
Factor Matrix Comparing Iowa/Washington
Factor Scores (second-order factor analysis)

	Factor		
	A	B	C
Iowa Factor 1	.50	−.16	.75
Iowa Factor 2	.40	.84	.27
Iowa Factor 3	.80	−.15	.13
Washington Factor 1	−.05	.14	.95
Washington Factor 2	−.22	.93	.13
Washington Factor 3	.92	.22	.03

Loadings +/−.33 significant p<.01

sets of factors is, by any standard, quite substantial (also see Brown and Coke, 1977, for a similar discussion of P-set/factor comparisons).

Findings: "Three Faces" of American Civil Religion

Turning, finally, to the factors themselves, the first thing to note is that these varieties of civil religion bear a striking resemblance to three of the four categories identified by Marty (1974). While his "Nation-as-Transcendent: Priestly"-type did not match any of our factors, the correspondence between the other categories and our findings is sufficient to warrant use of Marty's titles in labeling the factors.[5] Accordingly, the three civil religious orientations are identified as:

Factor 1: Nation-as-Transcendent: Prophetic
Factor 2: Nation-Under-God: Priestly
Factor 3: Nation-Under-God: Prophetic

Factor 1: Transcendent Nation: Prophetic. This view takes strong exception with the claim that America is God's agent. The discomfort aroused by such "priestly" pretensions is revealed most clearly in the negative valence of factor scores for items of this nature. (Iowa factor scores appear first in parentheses, followed by those from Washington.)

38. No people can be bound to acknowledge and adore the Invisible Hand that conducts the affairs of man more than those of the U.S. Every step . . . seems to have been distinguished by some token of providential agency. (–3, –4)

17. Conceived in justice, written in liberty, bound in Union, the United States was meant one day to inspire the hopes of all mankind. (0, –4)

Likewise, a Reaganesque civil theology, which holds that the United States should be a moral policeman to the world, is vehemently rejected:

27. I've always believed that this land was placed between the two great oceans by some divine plan to be found by a special people . . . who had a special love for freedom and . . . the courage to uproot themselves and come to what was the most underdeveloped wilderness possible. (–4, –4)

47. This nation is a chosen instrument of God, and it carries the major responsibility of implementing God's will in the world. (–5, –5)

18. We Americans are the peculiar, chosen people—the Israel of our time; we bear the ark of the liberties of the world. (–4, –5)

The "prophetic" character of Factor 1, on the other hand, is demonstrated by its strong endorsement of the statement: "When a nation is very powerful and feels it has God's blessing, it is likely to behave in a manner that is dangerous both to itself and to others" (+5, +5). The same theme is reiterated, again negatively, in reaction to a remark made by Dwight Eisenhower: "America is the mightiest power God has yet seen fit to put on His footstool. America is great because she is good" (−5, −5).

The view from Factor 1, however, is not simplistic. Although Factor 1 generally is liberal, as the statement scores above suggest, the Iowa sample is more "secular" whereas the Washington respondents affirm a more explicitly religious orientation. The differences that derive from this contrast are ones of emphasis and are best appreciated by comparing factor scores distinguishing the two samples. Thus Factor 1-Washington, despite its opposition to the marriage of God and America, maintains that a sense of the sacred is essential to political understandings.

> 40. Society is never merely a social contract, an association of individuals who band together out of mutual self-interest. It always transcends the social and finds its meaning in the sacred. (0, +2)
>
> 16. The rights of man come not from the generosity of the state but from the hand of God. (−2, +3)

It would seem that the religious component of Factor 1-Washington heeds a call to Christian activism, while embracing a neo-Burkean conservative view of society as an organic entity. That is, its prophetic aspect, though shared with Iowa, is qualified by a rejection of liberal social contract theory (statement 40) in favor of a covenant between God and his people (16). Thus the Washington variation allows for—indeed, calls for—Christian evangelicals to engage actively in politics. Factor 1-Iowa, on the other hand, maintains a liberal, "strict separationist" position with respect to church and state relationships.

> 25. I have thought for a long time that too many of our churches are too reluctant to speak up in behalf of what they believe is proper in government. (− 1, +4)
>
> 34. It's time for God's people to come out of the closet and the churches and change America. (−1, +3)
>
> 26. Christians have a God-given responsibility to be politically active. (−4, −1)

Continuation of the last statement asserts that Christians must dismiss from office those who have enacted mistaken liberal programs. The agreement of Washingtonians is most likely with the initial admonition that Christians be active: Its neutral placement in the overall factor array reflects a reluctance to dissociate with liberalism. This interpretation is supported by Factor 1's disagreement, in both samples, with the proposition that "liberals are the ones who have driven us into this current dilemma by trying to purge American life of religion and values" (–5, –2).

Finally, Factor 1 respondents in both locales are distinguished from the other factors by their fundamental rejection of the Moral Majority. They deny, for example, that Falwell's version of the gospel, if enacted, would lead to better and cleaner government. To the contrary, they see groups like the Moral Majority as guilty of poisoning civic life with an air of severe politico-religious rigidity. When complex political issues are reduced to a small number of moral absolutes, as they are by Falwellian fundamentalists, according to Factor 1, the result is a self-righteous, true-believing style that invites intolerance, begets dogmatism, and brands as "evil" anyone who would see matters differently.

Factor 2: Nation-Under-God: Priestly. In contrast to Factor 1, a specifically religious and stridently pro-America orientation permeates the perspective of Factor 2. It also stands in contradistinction to Factor 3, for which religion is salient but in a more critical and prophetic sense. The defining features of Factor 2 are its fundamentalist theology, conservative view of politics, and wholesale support for the Moral Majority.

Christians are called to political action but with a fundamentalist mission. Accordingly, Factor 2 rejects negative references to political involvement by fundamentalists, identifying with the latter in opposition to the demon of "secular humanism" and the mistaken public policies it has allegedly sustained. This theme, as indicated by scores for statements that follow, is more pronounced among Washingtonians defining Factor 2.

43. America is suffering from moral decay that, if not stopped, will end in the fall of the country. . . . Sin and its symptoms are dangerously real in this country, and these symptoms stem basically from a misguided philosophy some have called "secular humanism." (0, +3)

37. The ultimate end of secular humanism . . . is going to be the wipeout of the family and the destruction of all the traditional values that have made the U.S. the greatest free society in the world. (0, +4)

36. The radical right's crusaders seek to restrict our channels of communication by censoring anything that they view as porno-graphic, deprive women of equal rights by opposing the ERA, prohibit freedom of choice for the termination of pregnancies, limit

the rights of children, and harass adults for nonconventional sexual preferences. (–3, –4)

That this is a "nation-*under*-God" (not a "nation-as-transcendent") viewpoint is indicated by the scores of several statements speaking to the primacy of religious over political convictions. The latter, in contrast to the way a full-fledged "transcendent priestly" type would have it, must always remain subservient to the former. Hence, "the rights of man come not from the generosity of the state but from the hand of God" (+5, +5).

13. Morality can be maintained without religion. (–5, –4)

22. Reason and experience both forbid us to expect that national morality can prevail in the absence of religious principle. (+1, +4)

These last two statements point to a "Rousseauean" appreciation for the functional role of religious commitments in civil society. What is *not* Rousseauean in Factor 2, however, is the *nature* of this religious commitment: It is not "purely civil" at all. On the contrary, it is erected upon strong theological foundations. "The long road to survival," as the issue is put in part by statement 19, "lies in the Bible—not the ballot box" (+2, +4). God and nation may be conjoined, as the concept of civil religion implies they must, but the conjunction is clearly one of the polity placed *under* God.

42. It bothers me that there are those who speak presumptuously about our putting God back in government, rather than recognizing that God is always there, and that our task is to join in God's redemptive work. (+4, +1)

6. There is a great hunger in America for a spiritual revival, for a belief that law must be based on a higher law, for a return to traditions and values we once had. Our government, in its most sacred documents, the Constitution and the Declaration of Independence, speak of man being created, of a creator, that we are a nation under God. (+3, +4)

The latter comment, made by Ronald Reagan in 1980, might well be construed to have "transcendent priestly" connotations, and there is little doubt that Factor 2 is priestly by virtue of its celebration and affirmation of the American experience. But, contrary to critical portrayals, Reagan's version of American civil religion is one that stops short of unmitigated nation worship. Americanism and feelings of national pride may be in order, but such sentiments are warranted only so long as the nation's spiritual house is in order. With a kindred spirit occupying the White House, for the time being at least, this proviso is met for Factor 2. In any case, the brand of Americanism touted by such persons rests, theologically, on the "blessed considerable assurances that God is really in control." (+4, +5)

Factor 3: Nation-Under-God: Prophetic. Factor 3 shares with Factor 1 a critical and somewhat liberal view, and this political stance, as with Factor 2, is very much informed by religious understandings. The religious underpinnings of Factor 3, however, differ substantially from the Christian fundamentalism of Factor 2. Unlike the latter, it takes the prophetic position with high regard for transcendent values that serve to call the nation to humility rather than priestly celebration.

The factor's liberalism is found in support for liberal policies and rejection of the notion that liberalism is the bane of American society. Contrary to conservative claims, liberalism has not depleted traditional values.

12. Liberals who propound the separation of church and state have gone beyond that to the separation of moral judgment from public policy. (−5, −3)

28. Liberals are the ones who have driven us into this dilemma. (−4, −4)

Factor 3's animosity toward the religious New Right extends well beyond a defensive reaction to the latter's disdain for the twin symbols of liberalism and secular humanism. The extent of this animosity can be gleaned, initially, by the extreme disagreement with statement 54: "The Moral Majority is not a group of religious fanatics who have in mind a Khomeini-type religious crusade to take over the government" (−4, + 4). Further evidence to this effect is to be found in statements such as the following:

3. Jerry Falwell preaches the Gospel. He is against homosexual rights, pornography. . . . If the things he is for were included . . . and the things he's against cut out, there's no doubt that our government would be a lot cleaner. (−5, −3)

5. The really annoying thing about groups like the Moral Majority is that they divide us by denying their own humanness . . . excluding those who don't believe as they do. (+4, +4)

33. The so-called evangelical right seems to be less interested in attacking public evils than in legislating private morality. (+2, +2)

Open contempt for the intent and tactics of Christian fundamentalists, however, does not lead Factor 3 to abandon religious values. Instead, Christians are admonished to approach the politico-religious realm with a certain sense of "fear and trembling" by tolerating the ambiguities of Christian faith but distinguishing them from fundamental themes (God's love for the world, His power to rule over and redeem it—item 31 [+4, +1]).

Thus construed, religious convictions for Factor 3 offer an important frame of reference from which to approach the political order. The two samples vary somewhat, however, in their perceptions of how such religious values are to be applied. Hence Washingtonians agreed (+2) with Reagan's assertion, alluded to earlier, that "religious people have not only a right but a responsibility to speak out," whereas Iowans disagreed (−3). They concur, however, on the article of faith that America's salvation is arrived at via a Biblical as opposed to a political electoral route: (statement 19, noted above, received scores of +5 and +3).

The criterial issues, it seems, are moral vision and God's grace—not supporting religion per se. Both samples are irritated with "those who speak presumptuously about our putting God back into government, rather than recognizing that God is always there, and that our task is to join in God's redemptive work" (+2, +4). Redemption requires humility in the face of moral complexities and hence admission that one's own positions may not always be right:

41. Christians, of whatever denominational stripe, are never altogether right. Self-righteousness is the great temptation of religious people in politics. The political world needs humility as well as conviction. Christians have reason to supply both. (+2, +4)

44. As Christians of diverse political orientations, we need humbly to admit that we are not always able to discern God's will . . . as we face crucial policy choices. All groups of Christians must refrain from the arrogance of presumed omniscience and adopt instead an attitude of humility befitting our sinful nature. (+4, +2)

Finally, there is an element of hope, buttressed by a belief in God's promise *to* America. Patriotic sentiments arc not precluded but the spirit of allegiance is very much conditional, indeed covenantal, in character.

17. Conceived in justice, written in liberty . . . the United States was

meant to one day inspire the hopes of all mankind; and it binds us still. If we keep its terms, we shall flourish. (+3, +3)

23. For 200 years we've lived in the future, believing that America would be better tomorrow than today and today would be better than yesterday. . . . Together we can begin the world over again. We can meet our destiny and that destiny can build a land here that will be for all mankind a shining city on the hill. (+5, +4)

This last statement, a frequent refrain of Ronald Reagan before his election in 1980, might seem out of place in the *prophetic* civil religion of Factor 3. When read in the context of its broader configuration of civil religious beliefs, however, it can hardly be construed in "transcendent priestly" terms. Indeed, its endorsement in this connection casts its connotation in a much different light: Only a nation that first humbles itself is entitled to reap the blessings of God's handiwork.

Summary

In these interpretations we come full circle: Matters of meaning and significance are fundamentally self-referential. What a statement or a concept is supposed to signify a priori may vary considerably from the meanings of other parties to the conversation. In Q methodology, this is not a problem; indeed, it is axiomatic in as much as the factors that make up its chief empirical product remain fundamentally *operant (based on subject operations) and not categorical in nature.* As such, ascription of their meaning occurs only *after* their discovery and not before. Because the data are "public"—that is, others are free to examine the factor arrays and arrive at their own independent conclusions—our interpretations are open to debate. We view this circumstance as a virtue of the method; it raises important issues within the scientific community where it belongs—not over the quality of the data, but over the significance of their meanings.

In the complete report from which these findings are drawn, additional evidence is presented that corroborates the above interpretations. The varieties of civil religious experience display robust associations with a host of political-attitudinal (ideology, party identification), issue-position, and candidate-choice variables. Also included in the original study, omitted here for reasons of space, are discussions of (a) the issue of civil- religious consensus, (b) demographic differences that, suggestively at least, bear associations with the three faces of civil religion we find, and (c) numerous questions inevitably raised for further research.

STUDY 2: THE PERSONALITY-IDEOLOGY INTERFACE

Q, as we have stressed, is fundamentally a method for revealing the form and structure of operant subjectivity. As a final illustration of its applicability, we now turn to a research problem that calls for a slightly different combination of procedures than heretofore exemplified. Substantively, the concern is with the structure and form of ideological thinking and its relationship to human personality. The theoretical point of departure is provided by Tomkins's (1963) "polarity theory."

Theory

In broad outline, the theory postulates a fundamental distinction between two modes of thinking and valuing revealed over the course of Western philosophical controversy. According to Tomkins, these modes can be characterized as either *humanistic* ("leftwing") or *normative* ("rightwing") in nature, and one's resonance with one or the other is to be understood in terms of the position taken on the question: Are human beings ends in themselves, and thereby the creators of value, or do we strive to realize ourselves by conforming to objective norms that precede, transcend, and are independent of our existence? The humanistic (left), says Tomkins, resonates with the former while the normative (right) adheres to the latter. Tomkins further argues that one's initial stance in terms of this basic polarity in large part will determine the direction of later feelings and beliefs in such diverse areas as science, mathematics, politics, and child rearing.

Although he defines ideology as "any *organized* set of ideas about which human beings are at once both articulate and passionate and about which they are the least certain," Tomkins (1963: 389) does not preclude *unorganized, unarticulated feelings* from having any place in the polarity. In fact, it is his concept of ideo-affective postures (sets of loosely organized feelings or ideas about feelings) that he sees as the psychological foundation upon which the organized, articulate ideology is developed during socialization through a process he calls *ideo-affective resonance*. Through the latter process—which may be served, for example, by means of identification with a respected leader, group, or symbol—ideology engages more fundamental beliefs and feelings and becomes articulate and capable of intellectual expression, thereby assuming the properties of an ideology in the usual sense of the term. According to the resonance postulate, individuals with strong normative inclinations in one area, especially on the first polarity noted above, should be attracted to the norm-oriented alternatives in other areas as well. In other words, assuming a modicum of interest in the particular area of expression involved, an individual would not be expected to entertain rightwing beliefs in one context (e.g., human nature) and extreme leftwing beliefs in another (e.g., social control and conflict).

Variance Design Principles and Procedures

Tomkins's theory can be viewed instrumentally and reduced to its basic essentials in a completely randomized design, with two main effects in factorial arrangement, as shown in Figure 5.1. Following procedures described earlier (Section 2), this scheme was used to sample statements, most of them drawn from the polarity scale that Tomkins (1966) has developed, for each combination of the two main effects: (1) ideo-affective posture (2 levels) and (2) area of expression (6 levels). Replicating each of the 12 combinations five times, the result is a 60-item "Tomkins Q-sample."

Tomkins's theory is a manifestly categorical formulation of the structure and content of ideology. It is, of course, an empirical question whether or not his theoretical descriptions of left and right bear any affinities to the subjective predispositions of political actors. Of paramount import, therefore, is the operant subjectivity made manifest in the Q-sorting and the form and structure of this subjectivity as revealed in factor analysis. Be that as it may, on rare occasions, this being one, it is appropriate to regard the theoretical structure of a Q-sample as a hypothesis for testing, and to proceed, initially, by subjecting completed Q-sorts to analyses of variance. The point is to gauge the significance, in each case, of the postulated effects built into the factorial design.

In all, 72 nonrandomly selected respondents completed the Tomkins Q-sample by rank-ordering the items along a conventional Q-sort continuum from +5 (most agree) to –5 (most disagree). Also included were two additional Q-sorts, kindly provided by Professor Tomkins himself, in which he described how he felt an ideal "rightwing" and a "leftwing" respondent would each arrange the statements. Prior to correlation and factor analysis, each of the Q-sorts was subjected to a preliminary ANOVA for the aforementioned reason. A significant "between postures" effect was observed in 56 out of 72 cases, with follow-up tests indicating that "leftwing" statements were given significantly higher scores by 47 subjects, and "rightwing" items higher scores by 9 subjects. There is no claim that

Main Effects	Levels	
A. Postures	(a) Left	(b) Right
B. Areas of	(c) Human Nature	(d) Feelings
Expression	(e) Self-realization	(f) Interpersonal
	(g) Social Progress	Relations
	and Control	(h) Knowledge and
		Knowing

Figure 5.1: Design for Tomkins Q-Sample.

this procedure effects a "test" of Tomkins's theory. Nonetheless, the results help to identify subjects whose resonance with "left-" or "rightwing" themes is sufficiently pronounced to earmark them as possible "reference variates," as described below.

Theoretical Rotation

The $N - 72$ Q-sorts were correlated and factor analyzed (by both centroid and principal components methods for comparative purposes). Of the various alternatives, the two-factor principal components (unrotated) solution was deemed most satisfactory, as will be shown subsequently. Unlike earlier examples we have presented, factor rotation was performed manually in this case, *on the basis of theoretical considerations*. The rationale as well as mechanics for this procedure can be illustrated with reference to Figure 5.2, where the positions (loadings) of selected respondents are plotted in two-dimensional factor space. The Q-sorts of respondents 6 and 38 hold theoretical interest in light of the ANOVA results. By this measure, which is admittedly somewhat "external" by Q standards, these are the purest specimens of the left- and rightwing postures, respectively. These Q-sorts—that, incidentally, were uncorrelated ($r_{6.38} = -.06$)—were then treated as reference variates and factor rotation directed in such a way as to maximize, at the same time, the saturation of each on the factor with which it was associated. The end-result of all of this is a hand rotated, finalized version of the factor matrix, now consisting of the loadings of each Q-sort on Factor A' and Factor B'. The efficacy on this

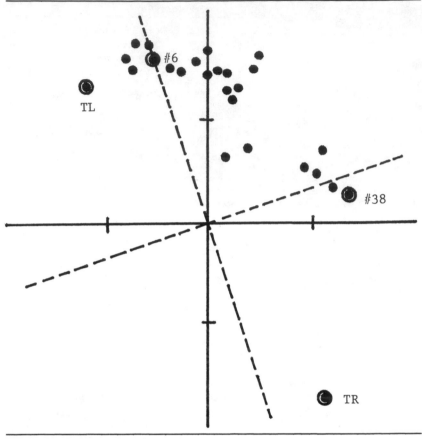

Figure 5.2: Graphic Depiction of Hand Rotation.

solution is indicated by the fact that only 3 of the 72 Q-sorts failed to have significant loadings on one and/or the other of these factors.

Left and Right as Operant Types

Space prohibits a detailed discussion, but a glimpse at the factor scores for 10 distinguishing statements reveals the general contours of the contrasting orientations of Factors A and B. (Scores for the former appear first in parentheses, followed by those for the latter.)

1. If there is anything like a divine spark in the human being, it is the faculty of reason by which he can control his passions and feelings. (–2, +3)

48. Human beings are basically good. (+4, –1)

32. To act on impulse occasionally makes life more interesting. (+4, +1)

30. Man must always leave himself open to his own feelings, alien as they may sometimes seem. (+3, –1)

42. For a human being to live a good life he must act like a good man, i.e., observe the rules of morality. (–1, +5)

59. The most important thing in the world is to know yourself and be yourself. (+5, –4)

53. For a human being to live a good life he must satisfy both himself and others. (+5, 0)

54. There are a great many things in the world that are good for human beings and that satisfy them in different ways. This makes the world an exciting and enriching place to live. (+3, –4)

10. A government should allow freedom of expression even though there is some risk in permitting it. (+4, +1)

60. The maintenance of law and order is the most important duty of any government. (–3, +3)

Taken contextually, these scores point up several similarities between the empirical types discovered here and Tomkins's categorical formulations. This convergence is corroborated as well when the respective factor arrays are subjected to variance analyses of the postulated effects structured into the Q-sample. The analyses showed the "between postures" effect for Factor A to be highly significant ($F = 70.69$; $df = 1, 46$; $p < .001$) and, as Figure 5.3 indicates, leftwing statements are assigned higher scores across all six areas of expression. A significant main effect did not materialize from the counterpart ANOVA for Factor B, although the pattern of means, as noted, is directionally consistent with expectations based on Tomkins's theory.

ANOVA results such as these, as we have noted, are of supplementary value only in Q-method. Though instructive, these data are useful primarily as aids in the contextual interpretation of factors, which relies most heavily on factor scores. When the latter are examined, it becomes clear that Factor A subscribes to a "self-referent" system of values, whereas

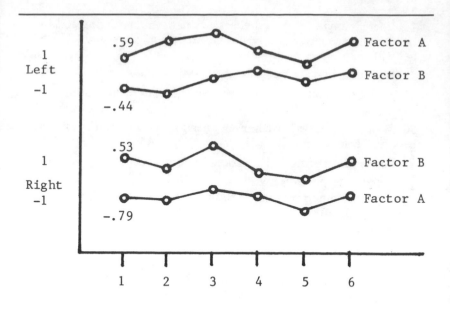

Figure 5.3: Left-Right Means for Factors A and B.

Factor B embraces a much more "norm-centered" position. In contrast to A's advocacy of self-indulgence and unbridled self-expression, for instance, Factor B recommends a restrained, disciplined route to self-realization. The same basic themes show up as well in such diverse topical domains as interpersonal relations, social control, and politics.

From these findings Tomkins's formulation would seem to have received considerable corroboration. His claim regarding the pervasiveness of the humanistic normative polarity is given credence by virtue of the efficiency of the two-factor solution. In addition, the twin poles of his ideo-affective dimension are seemingly substantiated in the *content* of each factor. Each expresses important themes that he attributes to his left and right prototypes. There are, however, important respects in which the findings deviate from expectations hypothetically deduced from Tomkins's theory. These deviations are deserving of brief comment since they illustrate the way in which Q is premised on a "logic of discovery" in which abductive inference figures prominently, as opposed to a "logic of confirmation" in which deduction is the governing mode of inference (see Stephenson, 1961a).

Ideo-Affective Structure: A Final Note

According to Tomkins, the structural relation of left and right is most aptly described as bipolar and because of this his theory is referred to as Tomkins's "polarity" theory. However, as a consequence of this unidimensional conceptualization, Tomkins was constrained, in designing an appropriate instrument of assessment, to construct a polarity scale capable of ordering individuals along a single continuum with left and right as opposite poles. Conceptually and operationally, such a procedure is not without limitations (Brown and Taylor, 1972; Conover and Feldman, 1984; De Soto, 1961; Marcus et al., 1974). If the assumption of bipolarity were tenable, it would have found corroboration in the discovery of one general factor with large numbers of defining variates at both the positive and negative poles. Such, however, was not the case. The structural relationship between left and right, depicted earlier in Figure 5.2, is *orthogonal* instead of bipolar. It is of considerable interest in this connection that the sole exception to orthogonality is found in the relationship between the two Q-sorts provided by Professor Tomkins himself. His Q-sort model of a prototypical leftwinger (designated "TL") is proximate to the Q-sorts of others on the leftwing Factor A; his hypothetical rightwinger ("TR"), on the other hand, occupies a position in factor space that is bipolar to the leftwing cluster. Tomkins's rightwinger, however, bears no perceptible relationship to—indeed, it varies randomly with respect to—the Q-sorts defining Factor B, all of which have earned the operant designation "rightwingers."

These findings raise serious questions about the accuracy of Tomkins's original portrait of ideo-affective rightwingers. The point is that the attribution of content to the normative posture is an unappreciated byproduct of the polarity assumption and the procedures by which it is made operational. What the leftwinger resonates with, the rightwinger must, *by definition,* reject. Because of polarity, the content of the two positions is conceptualized in terms of mirror images. The apparent accuracy of the leftwing attributions aside, the polarity postulate precludes the possibility in Tomkins's scheme of anything but a rightwing posture that is, ideologically, the "left in reverse." For Tomkins, in other words, ideological *content* (for the rightwinger, anyway) is a rather direct function of an ideological *structure,* the existence of which is assumed rather than demonstrated. (For a similar view of ideological structure—one that is based on Q-methodological practices—see Kerlinger, 1985.)

When permitted to model their views by operant means it is clear that those persons who opt for alternatives to "humanistic" values do so—and quite systematically—but *not* in terms of the"normative" inclinations identified by Tomkins. The rightwingers of Factor B (the affinities with Tomkins's type are sufficient to warrant the label) are not perceptibly worried or excited about the same concerns that engage those on the left. Indeed, that is the message of their orthogonal relationship as depicted earlier in two-dimensional factor space. Hence, while the right is clearly not comfortable with the leftwing's emphasis on self and impulse gratification, its "feelings about feelings" are considerably less intolerant, rigid, and inflexible, especially when relations with other people are involved, than Tomkins had hypothesized.

Thus the Q-data both support and qualify Tomkins's original formulation. Given the qualifications, it would appear that Tomkins's "polarity" theory may well be a misnomer. Left and right, it seems, are not opposite ends of the same polar spectrum at all, but independent (orthogonal) structures with differing "criterial referents" (Kerlinger, 1967, 1985) and areas of consensus as well as cleavage. As in the prior example, space precludes discussion of all of the findings and issues considered in full elsewhere (Thomas, 1976, 1978). Tersely reported though they are, these studies exemplify applications of the principles and procedures discussed earlier. We hope they are instructive in demonstrating the value of such applications as well.

6. KEY WORKS IN Q METHODOLOGY

Since Q methodology was first introduced by William Stephenson (1935), several primary treatments have been written discussing in detail its philosophical, technical, and statistical foundations. Stephenson's *The Study of Behavior* (1953b) remains the most complete statement of the method's psychometric principles and statistical foundations presented within the broader context of its distinctive logic of inquiry. In addition, Stephenson's *The Play Theory of Mass Communication* (1967) summarizes the methodological principles and offers several applications in studies of politics, journalism, and marketing. A concise treatment of the philosophical and psychological substructure is his three-part series first appearing in the *Psychological Record* (Stephenson, 1961a, 1961b, 1961c). A subsequent, extended statement of method, technique, and applications is Brown's (1980) *Political Subjectivity*. Broader methodological issues are also discussed at length, as are research applications in the social and communication sciences, in a collection of essays honoring the work of Professor Stephenson (Brown and Brenner, 1972). Especially noteworthy in this volume is Brown's essay, "A Fundamental Incommensurability between Objectivity and Subjectivity," which addresses the contrasting psychometric premises and principles of Q- and R-methodologies.

In a more introductory vein, Kerlinger's earlier (1972) overview of technical pragmatics remains useful, although silent on broader methodological issues. More helpful in the latter regard is Brown's (1986) brief characterization of Q as an alternative approach to measurement in the social sciences. Readers interested in pursuing particular research applications can find useful reviews by Dennis (1986) in connection with the helping sciences, by Stephen (1985) with regard to communication research, and by McKeown (1984) with reference to political psychology.

An extensive bibliography on Q methodology is available in Brown (1968). Continuing bibliographical updates of Q-based literature, including articles reporting original research as well as reviews of relevant methodological treatments, are a regular feature in *Operant Subjectivity: The Q Methodology Newsletter* (published quarterly at Kent State University under the editorship of Steven R. Brown).

NOTES

1. The letter "R" in this case signifies a generalization of Pearson's r, most often used in the behavioral study of relationships among analytically distinct traits, abilities, and the like.

2. The "meaning of the mean" is thus equivalent across persons in Q, a condition that does not often hold when traits, tests, and the like are correlated across people. When correlations are computed for variables within equivalent means and mean values are not reported, this information is lost by the normalization that correlational procedures subsume. More than that, correlational work with variables having nonequivalent means may produce statistically spurious and substantively nonsensical results, as Brown (1980: 14-15) shows.

3. In a sense, Q-method employs its own Grand Numbers. For example, in a study of Miller's (1972) reflections on competing philosophies of science, Brown (1978) estimates that "each subject at least implicitly had to consider each of the $N = 32$ philosophical propositions in relation to all others, leading to $\frac{1}{2}N(N-1) = 496$ comparative judgments per person— multiplied by 40 respondents—almost 20,000 acts of judgment in all" (p. 9). By the same token, one person performing the same Q-sort under 40 conditions of instruction makes an equal number of decisions.

4. Judgmental rotation thus would seek to maximize, to the extent that the data allowed, the loading of these respondents on a particular factor. This practice, illustrated more fully in Section 5, is analogous to "criterion analysis" in R-method (Eysenck, 1950).

5. The entire civil religion Q-sample and factor scores for both person-samples in this study are available upon request from the authors.

REFERENCES

ADCOCK, C. J. (1954) *Factorial Analysis for Nonmathematicians.* Melbourne: Melbourne University Press.

ANDERSON, N. H. (1968) "Likeableness ratings of 555 personality trait words." *Journal of Personality and Social Psychology* 9: 272-279.

ARNOLD, D. O. (1970) "Dimensional sampling: An approach for studying a small number of cases." *American Sociologist* 5: 147-150.

BAAS, L. R. (1979) "The Constitution as symbol: The interpersonal sources of meaning of a secondary symbol." *American Journal of Political Science* 23: 101-120.

BAAS, L. R. and S. R. BROWN (1973) "Generating rules for intensive analysis: The study of transformations." *Psychiatry* 36: 172-183.

BEEBE-CENTER, J. G. (1929) "The law of affective equilibrium." *American Journal of Psychology* 41: 54-69.

BELLAH, R. N. (1967) "Civil religion in America." *Daedalus* 96: 1-21.

BELLAH, R. N. and P. E. HAMMOND (1980) *Varieties of Civil Religion.* San Francisco: Harper & Row.

BLOCK, J. (1961) *The Q-sort Method in Personality Assessment and Psychiatric Research.* Springfield, IL: Charles C Thomas.

BOLLAND, J. M. (1985) "The search for structure: An alternative to the forced Q-sort technique." *Political Methodology* 11: 91-107.

BROWN, S. R. (1968) "Bibliography on Q technique and its methodology." *Perceptual and Motor Skills* 26: 587-613.

BROWN, S. R. (1970a) "Consistency and the persistence of ideology: Some experimental results." *Public Opinion Quarterly* 34: 60-68.

BROWN, S. R. (1970b) "On the use of variance designs in Q methodology." *Psychological Record* 20: 179-180.

BROWN, S. R. (1971) "The forced-free distinction in Q-technique." *Journal of Educational Measurement* 8: 283-287.

BROWN, S. R. (1972) "A fundamental incommensurability between objectivity and subjectivity." In S. R. Brown and D. J. Brenner (eds.) *Science, Psychology, and Communication.* New York: Teachers College Press.

BROWN, S. R. (1974a) "The composition of microcosms." *Policy Sciences* 5: 15-27.

BROWN, S. R. (1974b) "Intensive analysis in political research." *Political Methodology* 1: 1-25.

BROWN, S. R. (1974c) "The politics of self and others: Public reactions to the Kent State incident." In A. R. Wilcox (ed.) Public Opinion and Political Attitudes. New York: John Wiley.

BROWN, S. R. (1974d) "Significance of Q technique and its methodology for political science." Presented at the Midwest Political Science Association, Chicago.

BROWN, S. R. (1977) "Political literature and the response of the reader: Experimental studies of interpretation, imagery, and criticism." *American Political Science Review* 71: 567-584.

BROWN, S. R. (1978) "Intensive analysis in political research: Introductory comments." Presented at Midwest Political Science Association, Chicago.

BROWN, S. R. (1979) "Perspective, transfiguration, and equivalence in communication theory." In D. Nimmo (ed.) *Communication Yearbook 3.* New Brunswick, NJ: Transaction/International Communication Association.

BROWN, S. R. (1980) *Political Subjectivity*. New Haven: Yale University Press.

BROWN, S. R. (1981) "Intensive analysis." In D. D. Nimmo and K. R. Sanders (eds.) *Handbook of Political Communication.* Beverly Hills, CA: Sage.

BROWN, S. R. (1982) "Imagery, mood and the public expression of opinion." *Micropolitics* **2**: 153-173.

BROWN, S. R. (1983) "Monitoring the vicissitudes of mood." Presented at the Third International Symposium on Forecasting, Philadelphia.

BROWN, S. R. (1985) "Comments on 'The search for structure.'" *Political Methodology* **11**: 109-117.

BROWN, S. R. (1986) "Q technique and method." In W. D. Berry and M. S. Lewis-Beck (eds.) *New Tools for Social Scientists.* Beverly Hills, CA: Sage.

BROWN, S. R. (forthcoming) "Comments on 'The search for structure.'" *Political Methodology.*

BROWN, S. R. and D. J. BRENNER [eds.] (1972) *Science, Psychology, and Communication: Essays Honoring William Stephenson.* New York: Teachers College Press.

BROWN, S. R. and J. G. COKE (1977) Public Opinion on Land Use Regulation. Urban and Regional Development Series No. 1. Columbus, OH: Academy for Contemporary Problems.

BROWN, S. R. and J. D. ELLITHORP (1970) "Emotional experiences in groups: The case of the McCarthy phenomenon." *American Political Science Review* **64**: 349-366.

BROWN, S. R. and A. ROTHENBERG (1976) "The analysis of group episodes." *Small Group Behavior* **7**: 287-306.

BROWN, S. R. and R. W. TAYLOR (1972) "Perspective in concept formation." *Social Science Quarterly* **52**: 852-860.

BRUNNER, R. D. (1977) "An 'intentional' alternative to public opinion research." *American Journal of Political Science* **21**: 435-464.

BRUNSWICK, E. (1956) *Perception and the Representative Design of Psychological Experiments.* Berkeley: University of California Press.

BURT, C. (1940) *The Factors of the Mind.* London: University of London Press.

BURT, C. (1972) "The reciprocity principle." In S. R. Brown and D. J. Brenner (eds.) *Science, Psychology, and Communication.* New York: Teachers College Press.

BUTLER, J. M. (1972) "Self concept change in psychotherapy." In S. R. Brown and D. J. Brenner (eds.) *Science, Psychology, and Communication.* New York: Teachers College Press.

BUTLER, J. M. and G. V. HAIGH (1954) "Changes in the relationship between self-concepts and ideal concepts consequent upon client-centered counseling." In C. R. Rogers and R. Dymond (eds.) *Psychotherapy and Personality Change.* Chicago: University of Chicago Press.

CARLSON, J. M. and M. S. HYDE (1984) "Situations and party activist role orientations: A Q study." *Micropolitics* **3**: 441-464.

CARTWRIGHT, R. D. (1972) "The Q method and the intrapersonal world." In S. R. Brown and D. J. Brenner (eds.) *Science, Psychology, and Communication.* New York: Teachers College Press.

CONOVER, P. J. and S. FELDMAN (1984) "The structure of issue positions: Beyond liberal-conservative constraint." *Micropolitics* **3**: 281-308.

CONVERSE, P. E. (1964) "The nature of belief systems in mass publics." In D. E. Apter (ed.) *Ideology and Discontent.* New York: Free Press.

COTTLE, C. E. and B. F. McKEOWN (1981) "The forced-free distinction in Q-technique: A note on unused categories in the Q sort continuum." *Operant Subjectivity* 3: 58-63.

CREASER, J. W. (1955) "An aid in calculating Q-sort factor arrays. " *Journal of Clinical Psychology* 11: 195-196.

DENNIS, K. E. (1986) "Q methodology: Relevance and application to nursing research." *Advances in Nursing Science* 8: 6-17.

DE SOTO, C. B. (1961) "The predilection for single ordering." *Journal of Abnormal and Social Psychology* 62: 16-23.

EYSENCK, H. J. (1950) "Criterion analysis—an application of the hypothetico-deductive method to factor analysis." *Psychological Review* 57: 38-53.

GLAZER, B. G. and A. L. STRAUSS (1967) *The Discovery of Grounded Theory.* Chicago: Aldine.

GOLDMAN, I. (1984) "Communication and culture: A Q-methodological study of psychosocial meanings from photographs in Time magazine." Ph.D. thesis, University of Iowa.

HARMAN, H. H. (1976) *Modern Factor Analysis.* 3rd ed. Chicago: University of Chicago Press.

HOFFERBERT, R. I. and I. SHARKANSKY [eds.] (1971) *State and Urban Politics.* Boston: Little, Brown.

HUGHES, R. T. (1980) "Civil religion, the theology of the republic, and free church tradition." *Journal of Church and State* 22: 75-87.

KENISTON, K. (1968) *Young Radicals.* New York: Harcourt, Brace & World.

KENISTON, K. (1973) *Radicals and Militants.* Lexington, MA: D. C. Heath.

KERLINGER, F. N. (1967) "Social attitudes and their criterial referents: A structural theory." *Psychological Review* 74: 110-122.

KERLINGER, F. N. (1972) "Q methodology in behavioral research." In S. R. Brown and D. J. Brenner (eds.) *Science, Psychology, and Communication.* New York: Teachers College Press.

KERLINGER, F. N. (1985) *Liberalism and Conservatism.* Hillsdale, NJ: Lawrence Erlbaum.

KIM, J-O and C. W. MUELLER (1978a) "Introduction to factor analysis." Sage University Paper series on Quantitative Applications in the Social Sciences, 07013. Beverly Hills, CA: Sage.

KIM, J-O and C. W. MUELLER (1978b) "Factor analysis: Statistical methods and practical issues." Sage University Paper series on Quantitative Applications in the Social Sciences, 07014. Beverly Hills, CA: Sage.

KINSEY, D. and R. W. TAYLOR (1982) "Some meanings of political cartoons." *Operant Subjectivity* 5: 107-114.

LAING, R. D., H. PHILLIPSON, and A. R. LEE (1966) *Interpersonal Perception: A Theory and Method of Research.* London: Tavistock.

LANE, R. (1962) *Political Ideology.* New York: Free Press.

LASSWELL, H. D. (1930) *Psychopathology and Politics.* Chicago: University of Chicago Press.

LASSWELL, H. D. (1932) "The triple-appeal principle: A contribution of psychoanalysis to political and social science." *American Journal of Sociology* 37: 523-538.

LASSWELL, H. D. (1938) "Intensive and extensive modes of observing the personality-culture manifold." *Yenching Journal of Social Studies* 1: 72-86.

LINDER, R. D. and R. V. PIERARD (1978) *Twilight of the Saints.* Downers Grove, IL: Inter-Varsity Press.

80

LORR, M., P. DASTON, and I. SMITH (1967) "An analysis of mood states." *Educational and Psychological Measurement* 27: 89-96.

LUNDBERG, G. (1941) "Case studies vs. statistical methods—an issue based on misunderstanding." *Sociometry* 4: 379-383.

MARCUS, G. E., D. TABB, and J. L. SULLIVAN (1974) "The application of individual differences scaling to measurement of political ideologies." *American Journal of Political Science* 18: 405-420.

MARMOR, J. (1968) "The psychodynamics of political extremism." *American Journal of Psychotherapy* 22: 560-568.

MARTIN, R. and R. TAYLOR (1978) "Political obligation: An experimental approach." *Operant Subjectivity* 1: 61-69.

MARTY, M. E. (1974) "Two kinds of two kinds of civil religion." In R. E. Richey and D. G. Jones (eds.) *American Civil Religion.* New York: Harper & Row.

McKEOWN, B. F. (1977) "Identification and projection in religious belief: A Q-technique study of psychoanalytic theory." In T. Shapiro (ed.) *Psychoanalysis and Contemporary Science.* Vol. 5. New York: International Universities Press.

McKEOWN, B. F. (1978) "Displacement effects of hypnotically-induced mood states upon perception of public symbols." Presented at the Midwest Political Science Association, Chicago.

McKEOWN, B. F. (1984) "Q methodology in political psychology: Theory and technique in psychoanalytic applications." *Political Psychology* 5: 415-436.

McKEOWN, B. F. and R. CRAIG (1978) "The impact on student attitudes and perceptions of living and learning in another culture: A Mexican experience." Presented at the International Studies Association, Washington, D.C.

McKEOWN, B. F. and D. B. THOMAS (1985) "On the varieties of civil religious experience: Attitudinal dimensions of merging religion and politics." Presented at the Western Political Science Association, Las Vegas.

MEAD, S. E. (1975) *The Nation with the Soul of a Church.* New York: Harper & Row.

MEISSNER, W. W. (1974) "Portrait of a rebel as a young man." *International Journal of Psychoanalytic Psychotherapy* 3: 456-482.

MILLER, E. F. (1972) "Positivism, historicism, and political inquiry." *American Political Science Review* 66: 796-817.

NIE, N., C. H. HULL, J. G. JENKINS, K. STEINBRENNER, and D. H. BRENT (1975) *SPSS: Statistical Package for the Social Sciences.* 2nd ed. New York: McGraw-Hill.

NIEBUHR, R. (1944) *The Children of Light and the Children of Darkness.* New York: Scribner's.

NISBET, R. (1953) *The Quest for Community.* New York: Oxford University Press.

NOWLIS, V. (1965) "Research with mood adjective checklist." In S. Tomkins and C. Izard (eds.) *Affect, Cognition, and Personality.* New York: Springer.

REICH, C. A. (1971) *The Greening of America.* New York: Bantam.

RICKS, D. F. (1972) "Dimensions in life space: Factor analytic cases." In S. R. Brown and D. J. Brenner (eds.) *Science, Psychology, and Communication.* New York: Teachers College Press.

ROTHMAN, S. and S. R. LICHTER (1982) *Roots of Radicalism: Jews, Christians, and the New Left.* New York: Oxford University Press.

RUMMEL, R. J. (1970) *Applied Factor Analysis.* Evanston, IL: Northwestern University Press.

RUSSETT, B. (1971) "An empirical typology of international military alliances." *Midwest Journal of Political Science* 15: 262-289.

SKINNER, B. F. (1969) *Contingencies of Reinforcement.* New York: Appleton-Century-Crofts.

SMIDT, C. (1980) "Civil religious orientations and children's perceptions of political authority." Presented at the Midwest Political Science Association, Chicago.

SPEARMAN, C. (1927) *The Abilities of Man.* New York: Macmillan.

STEPHEN, T. D. (1985) "Q-methodology in communication research. " *Communication Quarterly* 33: 193-208.

STEPHENSON, W. (1935) "Technique of factor analysis." *Nature* 136: 297.

STEPHENSON, W. (1953a) "Postulates of behaviorism." *Philosophy of Science* 20: 110-120.

STEPHENSON, W. (1953b) *The Study of Behavior.* Chicago: University of Chicago Press.

STEPHENSON, W. (1961a) "Scientific creed—1961: Philosophical credo." *Psychological Record* 11: 1-8.

STEPHENSON, W. (1961b) "Scientific creed—1961: Abductory principles." *Psychological Record* 11: 9-17.

STEPHENSON, W. (1961c) "Scientific creed—1961: The centrality of self." *Psychological Record* 11: 18-25.

STEPHENSON, W. (1967) *The Play Theory of Mass Communication.* Chicago: University of Chicago Press.

STEPHENSON, W. (1970-1980) "Quiddity college." University of Missouri, Columbia. (mimeo)

STEPHENSON, W. (1974) "Methodology of single case studies." *Journal of Operational Psychiatry* 5: 3-16.

STEPHENSON, W. (1978a) "Applications of communication theory: IV. Immediate experience of movies." *Operant Subjectivity* 1: 96-116.

STEPHENSON, W. (1978b) "Concourse theory of communication." *Communication* 3: 21-40.

STEPHENSON, W. (1985) "Perspectives on Q methodology: IV. Behavioral worlds." *Operant Subjectivity* 8: 83-87.

STEPHENSON, W. (1986) "Protoconcursus: The concourse theory of communication." Parts I and II. *Operant Subjectivity* 9: 37-58, 73-96.

SUPPASARN, P. and R. C. ADAMS (1984) "Some discrete views of televised violence." *Operant Subjectivity* 7: 37-55.

THOMAS, D. B. (1976) "Exploring the personality-ideology interface: Q-sort consideration of Tomkins' polarity theory." *Experimental Study of Politics* 5: 47-87.

THOMAS, D. B. (1978) "Political belief systems and ideo-affective resonance: The structuring principle revisited." *Experimental Study of Politics* 6: 34-89.

THOMAS, D. B. (1979) "Psychodynamics, symbolism, and socialization." *Political Behavior* 1: 243-268.

THOMAS, D. B. and L. SIGELMAN (1984) "Presidential identification and policy leadership: Experimental evidence on the Reagan case." *Policy Studies Journal* 12: 663-675.

THOMAS, D. B., L. SIGELMAN, and L. R. BAAS (1984) "Public evaluations of the president: Policy, partisan, and 'personal' determinants." *Political Psychology* 5: 531-542.

THOMAS, D.B., R. MARTIN, R. W. TAYLOR, and L. R. BAAS (1984) "Moral reasoning and political obligation: Cognitive developmental correlates of orientations toward law and civil disobedience." *International Journal of Political Education* 6: 223-244.

82

THOMPSON, J. W. (1962) "Meaningful and unmeaningful rotation of factors." *Psychological Bulletin* 59: 211-223.

TOMKINS, S. S. (1963) "Left and right: A basic dimension of ideology and personality." In R. W. White (ed.) *The Study of Lives.* New York: Atherton.

TOMKINS, S. S. (1965) "Affect and the psychology of knowledge." In S. S. Tomkins and C. E. Izard (eds.) *Affect, Cognition, and Personality.* New York: Springer.

TOMKINS, S. S. (1966) *Polarity Scale.* New York: Springer.

WALLENSTEIN, M. H. (1976) "Political poster appeal: A partial audience typology." Master's thesis, Kent State University.

WIMBERLEY, R. C. (1976) "Testing the civil religion hypothesis." *Sociological Analysis* 37: 341-352.

WIMBERLEY, R. C. (1980) "Civil religion and the choice of president: Nixon in '72." *Social Forces* 59: 44-61.

WIMBERLEY, R. C., D. A. CLELLAND, T. C. HOOD, and C. M. LIPSEY (1976) "The civil religious dimension: Is it there?" *Social Forces* 54: 890-900.

ABOUT THE AUTHORS

BRUCE McKEOWN is Professor of Political Science at Seattle Pacific University, Seattle, Washington. His research interests are political theory, political psychology and sociology, and psychological metatheory. His articles have appeared in *Psychoanalysis and Contemporary Science, Journal of Psychology and Theology,* and *Political Psychology and Operant Subjectivity.*

DAN THOMAS is Professor of Political Science at Wartburg College, Waverly, Iowa. His principal research interests are in the areas of political psychology and the experimental study of political behavior. Among his publications are articles appearing in *Political Behavior, Experimental Study of Politics, Policy Studies Journal, Polity, American Politics Quarterly, Journal of Social Psychology, Journal of Applied Social Psychology,* and *Political Psychology.*

NOTES

NOTES

NOTES

NOTES

NOTES